Acknowledgments

The authors wish to acknowledge and express our enormous appreciation to those who assisted us in the development of this work. Most specifically, we recognize Mr. Gregory Good, Mrs. Patricia Amundson-Casservik, Mrs. Melinda Muller, and Mrs. Yvonne Fisher.

Four-Dimensional Leadership

The Individual, The Life Cycle, The Organization, The Community

William P. Fisher, Ph.D.

Christopher C. Muller, Ph.D.

PEARSON

Prentice
Hall

Upper Saddle River, New Jersey 07458

Library of Congress Cataloging-in-Publication Data
Fisher, William P.
  Four-dimensional leadership / by William P. Fisher & Christopher C. Muller.
    p. cm.
  Includes index.
  ISBN 0-13-109103-4 (pbk.)
    1. Leadership. 2. Organizational effectiveness. I. Muller, Christopher C. (Christopher
Craig) II. Title.

HD57.7.F583 2004
658.4'012—dc22   2004044587

> *To all aspiring leaders who have the good fortune of converting their leadership dreams into reality.*

Executive Editor: Vernon R. Anthony
Managing Editor: Mary Carnis
Production Editor: Heather Stratton Williams, GTS Graphics, Inc.
Director of Manufacturing and Production: Bruce Johnson
Manufacturing Manager: Ilene Sanford
Manufacturing Buyer: Cathleen Petersen
Creative Director: Cheryl Asherman
Cover Design Coordinator: Mary E. Siener
Cover Designer: Allen Gold
Cover Image: Getty
Senior Marketing Manager: Ryan DeGrote
Senior Marketing Coordinator: Elizabeth Farrell
Marketing Assistant: Les Roberts
Editorial Assistant: Beth Dyke
Compositor: GTS Graphics, Inc.

Pearson Education LTD.
Pearson Education Singapore, Pte. Ltd.
Pearson Education Canada, Ltd.
Pearson Education—Japan

Pearson Education Australia PTY, Limited
Pearson Education North Asia Ltd.
Pearson Educación de Mexico, S.A. de C.V.
Pearson Education Malaysia, Pte. Ltd.

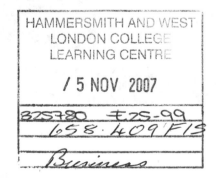

10 9 8 7 6 5 4 3 2 1
ISBN: 0-13-109103-4

Contents

■ ■ ■ ■ ■ ■ ■ ■ □ □

Preface

■　　■　　■　　■　　■　　■　　■　　■　　　□　　□

It is, perhaps, one of the most intriguing and engaging subjects in the realm of human interaction. It has been analyzed and generalized; assessed and professed; previewed, viewed, and reviewed; sought and bought; measured and treasured; proclaimed and exclaimed; exhalted and excoriated; conceived and perceived; renounced and redeemed; and appreciated and depreciated. The subject is LEADERSHIP.

Along with so many others, we have been long fascinated by this topic, but unlike so many of our colleagues and other mavens, past and present, our interest extends beyond a focus on the individual, as necessary as that is, to the leader in synthesis (or discordance) with an assembled framework to which we usually refer as an organization.

All organizations have life cycles, and matching the "right" leader-person at the appropriate stage of development of the organization can have a profound and lasting effect on the entity, for better or for worse. Whether this "match" is made in heaven, Gehenna, or somewhere in between can influence the course of events and the very survival (or demise) of the group. What are the factors that have a bearing on the mutual success or failure of the leader-person in juxtaposition with the entity he or she is leading?

We are also captivated by the concept that organizations, as constructs unto themselves (the so-called fictional being), can play an institutional leadership role in their industries and competitive environments, as well as in the communities where they operate. What are the characteristics of an organization that cause it to be the acknowledged, undisputed leader in its field of endeavor? Moreover, how do organizations relate to the larger society of which they are a part? Ignore it? Dabble in it? Embrace it?

These are the elements we seek to explore in this book. We know we don't have all the answers. We also know we do have some of them.

William P. Fisher, Ph.D.

Christopher C. Muller, Ph.D.

About the Authors

William P. Fisher, Ph.D.

Darden Eminent Scholar in
Restaurant Management
Rosen School of Hospitality Management
University of Central Florida

William P. Fisher, Ph.D. is the Darden Eminent Scholar in Restaurant Management at the Rosen School of Hospitality Management. Prior to joining the Rosen School, Dr. Fisher was the president and chief executive officer of the American Hotel & Lodging Association (AH&LA). He also served as the chief staff officer of the National Restaurant Association (NRA) and was the Executive Vice President for Finance and Administration for Service Systems Corporation.

Dr. Fisher holds three degrees from Cornell University: a bachelor of science from the School of Hotel Administration; an MBA; and a doctorate in educational administration. His academic credentials include serving as assistant professor at Cornell University's School of Hotel Administration, where he taught accounting, finance, and general management courses. Concurrent with his teaching responsibilities at Cornell, Dr. Fisher served as a hospitality industry consultant for Gaurnier Associates, a consulting firm serving the hotel and restaurant industries.

Dr. Fisher authored *Fisher's Laws: The Thinker's Guide to Management Action*, and has edited other books related to the hospitality industry. He was recognized with the

Champion of Education Award by the International Council on Hotel, Restaurant, and Institutional Education (CHRIE) in 1996, and received a Diplomate Award in 1998 from the National Restaurant Association's Educational Foundation.

Christopher C. Muller, Ph.D.
Associate Professor and Interim Director
Center for Multi-Unit Restaurant Management
University of Central Florida

Christopher Muller is a leading academic expert in the field of chain restaurant management. His research has focused on multi-unit restaurant brand management; chain restaurant organization development and growth; and the training of multi-unit managers.

Dr. Muller has lectured on these topics to a variety of individuals throughout the world, including presentations to groups from Germany, Great Britain, Italy, Singapore, Hong Kong, Korea, Australia, Central America, and Mexico. He is currently an associate professor in the Rosen School of Hospitality Management at the University of Central Florida, where he is the Interim Director for the newly created Center for Multi-Unit Restaurant Management.

Dr. Muller has had extensive experience in the hospitality service business. He has owned and operated restaurants and small hotels throughout New England; has worked in the international wine import and sales industry; and has served as a consultant to local, national, and international restaurant, beverage, and hospitality management companies. He has also served as an expert witness in a number of precedent-setting legal cases on topics ranging from restaurant trade dress and intellectual property, franchisee rights, and negligence issues.

Dr. Muller received both his doctorate and master's degrees from the School of Hotel Administration at Cornell University. His writings have been published in the *International Journal of Hospitality Management*, the *Cornell Hotel and Restaurant Administration Quarterly*, the *Journal of Hospitality & Tourism Research*, *FIU Hospitality Review, Foodservice Europe* , and the *Hospitality and Tourism Educator*.

Prologue

In every realm of human endeavor we hear common laments. "We need better leaders!" "We're lacking in leadership!" "We need new leadership as we face the future!" Perhaps you have uttered those sentiments yourself.

The recent wave of revelations of business wrongdoing brings that message to us in the daily headlines. Up until recently, had you ever heard of Enron, Global Crossing, Tyco, Adelphia, ImClone, or WorldCom? Well, maybe, but you probably never expected to hear about them in the context of financial malfeasance.

When you were young, did you ever hear about athletic coaches who falsified their resumes, clergy who were defrocked due to their horrendous transgressions, politicians who stepped away from their roles or were defeated in office due to admitted or uncovered sexual affairs, financial improprieties, or drug and alcohol abuse? Did you ever hear of researchers who falsified data to win acclaim or grant money? Did you ever hear of journalists who filed fabricated reports or union leaders who defrauded their members?

Once again, the answer is "maybe," but probably not with the constant bombardment of allegations, charges, indictments and convictions that permeate the airwaves and newswires today.

We don't claim to be as pure as Caesar's wife. However, we do claim to have studied, and to some extent lived a life of, leadership responsibility, which allows us to write this book on individual and organizational leadership.

Part I of this book, The Individual as the Leader, is devoted to aspects of individual leadership. The person who takes the reins of leadership requires a certain set of values, traits, qualities, skills, power bases and staying power to be a truly effective and memorable leader. People make up organizations, and so any discussion of leadership must start with the individual.

Part II of the book, Leadership: The Life Cycle, identifies the stages of growth and maturity of organizations (private and public, profit, and not-for-profit) and suggests the nature of individual leadership required to maximize the output measurements for any given cycle. The reason so many organizations fail is that there is an incongruity between what the leader brings to an organization and the type of leader that is in harmony with that cycle.

Part III, Leadership: The Organization, examines what is needed for organizational leadership to occur.

Part IV, Leadership: The Community, explores what many organizations do to participate in, contribute to, and play a leadership role in their local, national, and global communities. Most organizations contribute much more than many realize.

The title of the book is *Four-Dimensional Leadership*. Can we analyze and predict individuals and organizations that will be leaders? We think we can do a better job than has been done to date. That's our mission!

Part I

The Individual as the Leader

■　　■　　■　　■　　■　　■　　■　　■　　　□　　□

The emergence of leadership is founded on preparation and opportunity!
Christopher C. Muller, Ph.D.

Leadership is not forged in tranquility; it is forged in adversity!
William P. Fisher, Ph.D.

Leadership Defined and Undefined

"Leadership" is one of the most compelling, enigmatic, talked about, written about, complained about, envied and emulated concepts in the realm of human existence. It is mercurial, hard to define, but evident when we witness it. Everyone wants to possess it but few actually realize it. There are more "pretenders" than acknowledged leaders, and a historical perspective is necessary for a complete evaluation.
William P. Fisher, Ph.D.

There are as many definitions of leadership as there are people in the world. We each have our own concept of what leadership means.

1

Recognizing that there is no satisfactory, all-encompassing, and universally acceptable definition of leadership, we, nonetheless, develop our working model so that we can start from a common base. We are sure you can quibble with what follows, but we believe we have captured the essence of the concept.

Leadership is the art and science of continuous achievement and notable advancement in accomplishing the vision, goals, and objectives of a passionate constituency with the informed consent and the willful support of that constituency over a sustained period of time. (Note: There can be more than one constituency.)

We also find it useful to identify what leadership is not. Confusion abounds when discussions of leadership occur, because definitions can be imprecise, and words can be interpreted in multiple ways. The following descriptions encompass what we believe leadership not to be.

ADMINISTRATOR—is primarily charged with facilitating the flow of information, data, paperwork and soon, in an efficient and effective manner. An administrator is one cog in a wheel, not the wheel itself.

MANAGER—is primarily responsible for assembling and deploying resources (financial, human, property) together with establishing control systems and reward and discipline features. A manager does things correctly, but may not always do the correct things.

ENTREPRENEUR—has the creative energy and vision to take advantage of a situation and initiate activity but may not have the skills and qualities to oversee growth and expansion over the long term.

EXECUTIVE—taken literally, an executive's primary function is to execute, to take actions to see that something is done or undone. The word "executive" lacks the implication of requisite leadership provisions of vision, planning and strategy formation.

DIRECTOR—is one who has the primary responsibility to direct resources in optimal proportions and in appropriate channels, but the word "director" does not convey many of the virtues associated with leadership. It also can have an "authoritarian" connotation.

POSITIONSHIP—one who holds the topmost position is not necessarily the leader in the truest sense. Positionship is different from leadership in that the incumbent may be devoid of the traits, qualities, skills, and values necessary to assert leadership.

There are a number of other words (overseer, superintendent, supervisor, dictator, foreman, etc.), which suggest titles and positions, but leadership is vastly different from each of these. For example, we have all known position holders who were not considered leaders by their constituencies, and we have all known leaders who did not hold high positions but were the "looked-to," acknowledged leaders of their constituencies.

Much of the confusion surrounding the concept of leadership is that many of the values, qualities, traits, and skills necessary for an administrator, a manager, an executive, an entrepreneur, a director, or a position holder to function at high performance levels are also attributes of leaders. This overlap muddles rather than clarifies the true concept of leadership. It may be helpful to remember that leaders look outside as well as inside their organizations, while others, such as managers and administrators, are focused only on the mechanics of the organization, not its direction.

Perceptions of Leaders

Throughout history, leaders have been perceived by their followers in a variety of ways. We have named 20 types of leaders and their characteristics. You may not know all of the names or you may feel that we have misclassified a few, and you may well be right for a number of these people could fall into more than one category.

1. **DEITIES**

   Both the Greeks and the Romans had mythological gods, each possessing desirable virtues, such as wisdom, strength, and speed, to which humans could aspire. During the era of the Roman Empire, the Caesars were considered gods and regarded with that level of esteem by Roman citizens. Until the end of World War II, the occupant of the Japanese throne was deified by the Japanese people.

2. **WARRIORS**

   The great warriors in history were considered great leaders. They often were given this status because of their constituencies' fear to challenge them and a real or exaggerated reputation of martial success. Attila the Hun, Alexander the Great, Genghis Khan, and Napoleon are ancient examples. In more recent times, Dwight Eisenhower, Douglas MacArthur, George Patton, Erwin Rommel, and Norman Schwarzkopf are regarded as talented military leaders.

3. **HEROES/HEROINES**

   Persons known for monumental acts of courage and an almost spiritually infused fervor to overcome challenges and obstacles gain the status of heroes and heroines in the eyes of their constituencies. Their new status causes them to be perceived as leaders. Moses and Joan of Arc were two such individuals, as was Audie Murphy, the most decorated American soldier in World War II. Murphy received what is known as a "battlefield commission" due to his bravery and leadership abilities in a theater of war and later became a movie star. Charles Lindbergh and Amelia Earhart were heroes in their time. Today, in light of terrorist attacks, firefighters and police are seen as heroes and heroines.

4. THE WEALTHY CLASS

People of great financial wealth are often considered leaders, most likely because of the influence they wield based on their family assets. Vanderbilt, Rockefeller, Kennedy, DuPont, and Ford are familiar names that are associated with fortune, prominence, and leadership. Bill Gates currently falls in this category.

5. CHANGE AGENTS

People who cause seismic change in society or a field of endeavor are usually considered leaders. Consider the reverence Americans have for George Washington, Abraham Lincoln, and Franklin D. Roosevelt. Each of these presidents led the way for epic changes in times of national duress. Consider Notre Dame's Knute Rockne, father of the football forward pass, and Susan B. Anthony, a leader in securing the right to vote for women. These individuals were agents of irreversible change through their courage, vision, and leadership. Rosa Parks and Nelson Mandela are also considered leaders because of their monumental impact on race relations both in the United States and throughout the world.

6. FIGUREHEADS

Figureheads are often considered leaders due to tradition, role, heritage, and ceremony, even if their influence is strictly personal rather than institutional. Queen Elizabeth of England is a prime example, as are other monarchs throughout the world.

7. INTELLECTS

Philosophers, academicians, and even journalists are regarded as leaders by their constituencies. Socrates, Plato, Albert Einstein, Nobel Prize winners, and university presidents often have an impact and influence that extends well beyond their locality and field of endeavor.

8. COMMUNICATORS

Communicators are the people who speak to us with reliability and credibility. Former president Ronald Reagan was often referred to as "The Great Communicator." Walter Cronkite, the former anchor of the *CBS Evening News,* was once voted the most trustworthy man in the United States based on the believability of his reporting.

9. **NEGOTIATORS**

   Negotiators are frequently regarded as leaders, not only for their representative roles but also for their ability to work with all parties involved on an issue with trust and confidence. Colin Powell, Henry Kissinger, former president Jimmy Carter, and, on occasion, Jesse Jackson, assume the mantle of the office of negotiator.

10. **EXEMPLARS**

    Some people are elected or selected to their leadership roles as they represent the embodiment of a group's culture and values. Miss America, the Teacher of the Year, and Coach of the Year are a few such exemplars.

11. **TEACHERS**

    Leaders often are looked upon as outstanding, or at least memorable, teachers. They tell us the things we should know and prepare us for the future. Confucius, Jesus, and Mohammed are three such teachers whose influences reach into current times.

12. **INVENTORS**

    Those who make discoveries that benefit society are usually looked upon as leaders due to their brilliance and diligence in creating their inventions. Some well-known inventors are Benjamin Franklin; Thomas Edison; George Eastman, the father of photography; and Jonas Salk, the inventor of the polio vaccine.

13. **POLITICIANS/STATESPERSONS**

    By virtue of their governmental positions, politicians and statespersons have the label "leader" attached to them. Consider current world leaders but also consider past leaders, such as Winston Churchill, Harry S. Truman, Margaret Thatcher, and Willie Brandt.

14. **EXPLORERS**

    Those daring men and women who set about exploring the world acquire leadership acclaim. Marco Polo and Christopher Columbus made celebrated journeys, and Neil Armstrong will live in history as the first man to set foot on the moon. Fewer people may know of Cecil Rhodes and Lewis and Clark, but their expeditions opened new territories.

15. **EXPERTS**

    People considered experts in their fields of endeavor are surrounded by an aura of leadership. Their words are listened to very carefully and can affect world events. Consider in this regard Alan Greenspan, Bill Gates, Steven Spielberg, and Warren Buffet.

16. CRITICS

Sometimes it takes an outspoken critic of an existing situation or condition to generate change, even though that change may proceed at a glacier-like pace. Such change is usually beneficial and irreversible. Think of Martin Luther, Martin Luther King, Rachel Carson, and Nelson Mandela.

17. MOTIVATORS

Motivators are those persons who can instill, or cause others to instill in themselves, the drive to achieve remarkable success. Although their motivational and leadership styles are different, Billy Graham, Vince Lombardi, Phil Jackson, Teddy Roosevelt, and Dale Carnegie have all influenced others.

18. CREATORS

Creators have dreams and seek fulfillment of those dreams. Often they become legends in their industries and society, and their personal leadership transcends to their organizations. Consider Walt Disney; Willard Marriott, Sr.; Conrad Hilton; Ray Kroc; and Dave Thomas.

19. REWARDERS/PUNISHERS

These leaders are those who have resource control and can reward or punish members of a group or the entire group. Because they possess this power, they are (sometimes grudgingly) considered leaders. King Henry VIII of England actually beheaded five of his wives for failing to provide him with a male heir among other reasons. Walter Annenberg, a publishing giant, founded schools of journalism at two major American universities. William Randolph Hearst, another publishing giant, was also a benefactor to a number of causes and institutions.

20. SERVANT LEADER

Current discussions on leadership focus on the leader as servant of the constituency he or she serves (leads). One quality of this type of leader is humility. Mother Teresa is an example of a servant leader, as is Mahatma Gandhi. Servant leaders are responsible for developing leadership in subordinates so they can complete current assignments at a peak performance level and gain additional leadership responsibilities in the future.

We could add to this list by identifying more categories (visionaries, monitors, etc.) and by giving numerous examples of people who are known for those attributes. We will briefly return to these characteristics later, but it is necessary to understand that people perceive those characteristics to differentiate leaders from everyone else.

The Five Touchstones of Leader–Group Relations

In order to be successful, a leader must communicate with the inner core of his or her constituents. Such communication needs to be accomplished for each individual and with the group as a whole. As we will note later, a group has a persona different and apart from the aggregation of personalities of individual constituents.

There are five touchstones that underpin the relationship of a leader to the group, and vice versa. If a leader can convey positive answers to the unspoken inquiries of his or her followers, then that inner core can be reached.

1. **CAN I TRUST YOU?**

   All relationships are built on trust. Once trust is lost, it is rarely fully regained. A leader's trustworthiness is based on his or her integrity, character, honesty, credibility, and sincerity. It is the hallmark of the leader's relationship with the constituency.

2. **DO YOU RESPECT ME?**

   Everyone wants the respect of others. Successful leaders realize the value of self-respect and group respect and the necessity for honoring the dignity of the individual. Many "pretender" leaders delight in depersonalizing their subordinates and in shaming, embarrassing, undercutting, and demoralizing them, often as an exercise of their own egos. At some point, such "leaders" lose the respect and esteem of their constituencies and become despots and tyrants. A basic precept of leadership holds that the leader must bond with the group; we suggest that successful leaders pay as much attention to their common bonds as they do their common stock.

3. **ARE YOU INTERESTED IN MY WELL-BEING?**

   A leader is responsible for meeting the goals of the group but must also address the welfare of group members. These responsibilities often are thought of as task oriented and people oriented, respectively. In reality, of course, the successful leader integrates the two "poles" into a single style of leadership that accomplishes both objectives without sacrificing one for the other.

4. **DO YOU PRACTICE WHAT YOU PREACH?**

   Regrettably, a number of pretender leaders do not practice what they preach. Hypocrisy in a leadership context can cause an immediate downfall. Ask former Colorado senator Gary Hart or the televangelists who "sinned" while preaching spiritual and moral tenets. Successful leaders do not lapse in judgment or allow themselves to be placed in compromising positions. One principle media consultants impress on their clients who aspire to be leaders is that "there is no such thing as a dead microphone, a shuttered camera or a confidential conversation."

5. **ARE YOUR OBJECTIVES ACHIEVABLE?**
Followers want to believe that their leaders' objectives are realistic and attainable so they can have a sense of accomplishment, satisfaction, and fulfillment. A leader who sets unrealistic objectives quickly becomes a target for criticism and derision. This is not to say setbacks will not occur. "Course corrections" will be necessary, but successful leaders keep themselves and their groups focused, informed, and motivated.

Principles of Leadership

Given that the subject of leadership is somewhat ambiguous, and that it is only one element of a three-part dynamic consisting of the leader, the group, and the situation, there are few things one can say about it in absolute terms. However, there are a few identifiable bedrock principles.

1. **LEADERSHIP IS PERSONAL** Leadership is a uniquely human experience. Even though we often refer to the "lead dog" or the "lead horse," animals cannot lead. They may have a position in an alignment, but they cannot be leaders. Computers and signals do not lead. They can provide data that can be acted upon or can provide direction, as do traffic lights and road signs, but that is not leadership.

2. **LEADERSHIP IS BOTH AN ART AND A SCIENCE** Thought, judgment, and behavior are pieces of leadership that are subjective and emanate from within the individual (art). There are also some fundamental tenets of leadership that can be learned and are based on research and observation (science). For example, not criticizing an employee in front of others is a time-honored precept of practicing good leadership.

3. **A LEADER MUST HAVE A FOLLOWING** Leadership cannot exist in a vacuum; there must be interaction so that acts of leadership can occur. In an extreme example, a hermit could not be a leader, because his or her self-imposed isolation removes the possibility of human interaction. A lone shepherd tending sheep or a lone cowboy herding cattle would not be leaders, because people are not the followers.

4. **THERE IS NO SINGLE TRAIT, QUALITY, OR SKILL, OR BLEND OF SUCH, THAT WILL ALWAYS GUARANTEE LEADERSHIP** A great deal of research has been conducted to identify the skills, qualities, and traits of leaders to ascertain whether a single

element or blend of elements can predict, if not guarantee, leadership. Much of the research came out of World War II (you can imagine the military's interest in the subject), and several universities, most notably Ohio State University and the University of Southern California, continue to study the subject intensely. At this point, the only conclusion that can be drawn with certainty is that there is no skill, quality, trait, or combination thereof that will absolutely guarantee leadership. Life would be so much more simple, and perhaps less interesting, if such a discovery occurred.

5. **LEADERSHIP IS ONE ELEMENT OF A THREE-PART DYNAMIC; THE LEADER, THE GROUP, AND THE SITUATION ARE ALWAYS IN INTERACTION AND TENSION WITH ONE ANOTHER** These three elements are fluid and flexible, causing a constant dynamic tension in the leader's environment. Successful leaders are more adept at managing the group and the situation compared to their less successful counterparts.

6. **LEADERSHIP IS ACTIVE; LEADERS MUST DO SOMETHING** There is an expectation that the leader will orchestrate and activate resources to apply to the objective. This is not to say that the status quo must always be changed; sometimes making no change is a good decision. Over the long run, however, the leader is expected to be visibly active in pursuit of group objectives in order for the group to feel that positive movement is occurring.

7. **FOLLOWERS MUST FREELY ACCEPT LEADERSHIP EFFORTS FOR LEADERSHIP TO OCCUR** Followers must voluntarily align their will with that of the leader. Cajolery, seduction, or the threat of discipline or punishment does not constitute leadership, because they do not allow followers the full exercise of their free will. It is only when followers make a true choice to follow the leader that true leadership occurs.

8. **LEADERS KNOW THAT THE BEST DISCIPLINE IS SELF-DISCIPLINE, THE BEST CONTROL IS SELF-CONTROL, AND THE BEST EVALUATION IS HONEST SELF-EVALUATION** Leaders control resources. They can award or withhold compensation, bonuses, and options. They can provide praise, criticism, or silence. They can give delightful or difficult assignments. However, successful leaders know they must nurture trust in their followers and instill a passion for achievement and a determination to see things to a positive conclusion. They seek to imbue a culture of continuous self-improvement in themselves and their subordinates.

9. **LEADERS CREATE THE CAPACITY FOR ADAPTABILITY** Group members and situations often change; therefore, the successful leader must create the capacity, expectation, and confidence for

the changes that occur. Static leadership does not last long; consider the many organizations that were "superstars" years ago that no longer exist today.

Successful leaders are constantly thinking ahead, planning for the future, apprising subordinates of opportunities and exciting them as to the possibilities. Their enthusiasm is contagious.

We should now turn our attention to skills, qualities, and traits that leaders need to realize their full leadership potential.

Leadership Traits, Qualities, and Skills

Just as the word "leadership" has different meanings to different people, so, too, do the words "traits," "qualities," and "skills." Sometimes these words are used as synonyms; equally often, they are used to distinguish one feature of a person from another.

For example, most people believe that it is an asset for a leader to be a "listener." But is good listening a trait, quality, or skill? You could make a strong argument for any of the three terms. If "organizational ability" is a desired asset in a leader, do you consider it a skill, a trait, and/or a quality?

We will create distinctive definitions for these three words to help clarify what each is and as an aid in clarifying what leadership is (and is not).

Trait—a prominent, desirable physical or personality characteristic of a person.

Qualities—the outward manifestations of the values held by a person that cause that person to act (perform) in a certain way.

Skills—those refined or acquired abilities that allow a person to function in the world with a measurable degree of competence.

Essentially, traits describe how others view you; qualities describe how you define yourself; and skills describe the abilities you possess. Now that we have given definition and clarity to those words, lets employ them as we look at the needs of leaders.

TRAITS

No single combination of physical and/or personality traits has ever been identified that guarantees a person will be a leader with every type of group in every kind of situation.

Extensive research has identified some traits that are characteristic of leaders, but it's not foolproof and the absence of one, or the presence of another, is no guarantee of leadership. Nonetheless, it is instructive to know what those traits are so you can nurture them. Here are 12.

1. Intelligence—Successful leaders possess, and are perceived by group members to possess, an elevated degree of intelligence relative to the average intelligence of the group. However, group perceptions often confuse "possession of knowledge" with innate intelligence. Further, excessively superior intelligence on the part of a "leader" can result in ostracism, subterfuge, or bemusement by the group. Although it can sometimes work against you, demonstrated intelligence is generally an absolute requirement for leadership success.

2. Desire for excellence—Successful people possess a drive for perfection, a striving to reach beyond the ordinary to a level of astonishing achievement. This trait often manifests itself through an attention to detail. Frequently, this detail consciousness is perceived as "pickiness" by less perceptive subordinates, unless the broader foundations of personal and professional competence have been firmly laid by the leader and are demonstrated and reinforced on a continuing basis.

3. Conscientiousness—This is the conscious acceptance of the position's responsibility, the understanding of one's role in the organization, and the thoughtful use of authority. The conscientious leader will *delegate* in good faith, and will not *relegate* simply out of abdication or mental/physical necessity. Leaders are perceived willingly to put in more hours (and more into the hours) than the average group member, which is the tangible and visible evidence of the leader's acceptance, understanding, and commitment to the role and the organization.

4. Diligence—This is a fierce tenacity to attain both short-term and long-term objectives. The "stick-to-itiveness" exhibited by the leader allows the leader to focus resources rather than squander them. Leaders also recognize weak spots and losses before the average group member and are not timid to alter resources or reshape objectives in light of those circumstances.

5. High upward mobility drive—Leaders possess a high upward mobility drive. They want to be known as persons of impact, influence, and presence, and they view leadership as a means of accumulating increased amounts of responsibility channeled to defined organizational goals. They accept praise and adulation but are not affected by it except as a reinforcer of their mobility drive.

6. Self-confidence—Leaders have tremendous faith in their own abilities and judgment. They look to their own standards as a basis for their actions and are not swayed by bandwagon psychology or the "go-along-to-get-along" precept. Leaders are independent of, but not removed from, others; they rely on good eye contact and exhibit honesty, integrity, and the "habit of command." Leaders are not befuddled or immobilized by new situations; rather, they handle them directly and adeptly. They enjoy challenges.

7. Extroversion—Group members perceive successful leaders as freely mixing and mingling among them with no self-consciousness. Leaders are active persons, finding reward and enjoyment in personal interaction, and they contribute measurably to the facilitation of both professional and social communication interchange. Successful leaders who have risen from the ranks exude an air that sets them apart from—not necessarily above—the group of which they were once members.

8. Communication capability—This trait involves two elements. First, the successful leader is one who can view and summarize group thinking and sentiments quickly and accurately. Second, the leader is an individual who possesses more information than the average group member. A person holding such a position is at an advantage compared to those who have only a piece of the total picture. One who can distill a mélange of facts and feelings and summarize them in an articulate manner without diluting their complexity is in command of the situation.

9. Humor—Leaders have been found to possess a constructive sense of humor. They have the ability to laugh at themselves and do not feel threatened by the injection of appropriate humor. They are not overly intense, retaining the ability to step back from the situation and assess it with a fresh pair of eyes.

10. Team player—The group's perception of a leader is culturally based to some extent. The strong leader is expected to represent, through personification, action, and vocalization, the values and goals of the group. In this sense, the leader is the group's symbol and substance for which it stands. The leader is one of the group but is a "first among equals." The leader is not perceived to be manipulative of people, only of inanimate resources, and maintains constant attention and reference to the group's goals.

11. Planning—Leaders spend considerable time planning. Successful leaders plan for both the short range and the long range, continually relating aspects of the one to the other. The leader must be simultaneously shortsighted and farsighted. Planning gives purpose to the group and leaders know, and are perceived to know, where they are taking the group or organization.

12. Decisiveness—Leaders take decisive actions. They are not encumbered by self-doubt and do not reflect on regrets in hindsight. They know the hardest decisions of all are people decisions. This does not mean they act rashly, act on inadequate information, or remain rigidly committed to a course of action if subsequent events change. It does mean they set the direction and then move toward it, making "course corrections" as necessary.

QUALITIES

We now move on to examine leadership qualities. Allow us to set the stage and then we will address some essential qualities necessary for success.

Successful leadership rests on the elements of the leader, the group, and the situation that interact with one another. The group and the situation are often fluid—emerging, converging, diverging, resurging—in a cyclical and, hopefully, progressive pattern. The leader must recognize these stages of group and situation dynamics and bring skill, talent, and capabilities to bear on them. This is not to say the leader must be a chameleon, changing colors depending on one's mood. It does mean that a leader must call from his or her innermost personal resources that element or combination of elements in just the right proportion and with just the right degree of intensity, to draw the utmost from the group as it interfaces with the situation to achieve organizational goals.

Earlier we identified some key traits that successful leaders possess. We now go beyond that identification to determine the belief and behavior patterns successful leaders exhibit in their relationships with others.

1. Activation—Truly successful leaders are generous people, not necessarily in the financial sense but in recognizing that their talents, while residing in their person, in fact belong to the organizations they serve. The importance of their contributions and satisfactions is not the giving or receiving but the activating, for they know that it is through activity that expression and creativity give rise to organizational and personal development.

2. Competitiveness—The successful leader believes that success comes from competition and that competition does not, in the total sense, involve the destruction of competitors, but their own fortification and resolve, which, in turn, is stimulative and developmental to the organization. Successful leaders do not shrink from competition or challenge, but set their minds to conquer it.

3. Courage—The successful leader knows that success is the mastery of a situation, but that success is accompanied, however slight, by a fear of failure based on a possible change in the situation or a change in society's values of what is desirable. Because we cannot conquer unpredictability, we are forced to live with it. The leader does so with rationality, poise, professionalism, a secure confidence, an aura of courage, and a buoyancy of spirit.

4. Challenge—Successful leaders appreciate the complexity of their current decisions relative to the uncomplicated matters they may have faced earlier in their careers, when the right decisions seemed much more obvious. Yet, they do not require a crutch to escape complexity; they find enjoyment and solace in the analysis of the very factors that go into the decision-making process.

5. Simplicity—Leaders condense their organizational leadership roles into a relatively few fundamental operating notions. They are persons of recognized intellectual capability, and although detail conscious, they are not detail confined.

6. Trust—The successful leader possesses a guarded trust of others, having experienced both the joy of subordinates working to and beyond their capabilities and disappointment in human failings. The organization is viewed neither as a jungle nor as an infirmary but rather as an economic and social system of which the leader is a part and for which the leader has full responsibility.

7. Connectivity—Successful leaders are adept at seeing the interconnectedness of events that the average person sees only as isolated, unrelated incidents. Consequently, successful leaders have a mental framework for decision-making purposes that is simultaneously expansive and precise. Their ability to see and draw relationships among events that impact their organizations provides them with the "sixth sense" on which they can take action. They think both strategically and tactically.

8. Stewardship—True leaders develop a culture of leadership within their constituencies. They realize they have an obligation to the future and that it is incumbent on them to build and leave a legacy of leadership among their constituencies. They respect the past, lead in the present, and prepare for posterity.

SKILLS

1. Envisioning Possibilities—Leaders have developed creative thinking habits that allow them to envision possibilities of which others have not dreamed before. Sometimes those possibilities are extensions of current circumstances, and other times there is a quantum leap of brilliance that conceptualizes something truly new and unique. Leaders have the ability to translate their vision into more formalized planning that provides the blueprint for converting an idea into reality. Many leaders report that these visions of possibilities occur to them while they are sleeping, listening to music, or showering, or that they are following a train of thought when suddenly a lightening bolt strikes their consciousness, energizing them and compelling them to follow it to a conclusion.

2. Organizing—Leaders have a sense of the resources they need to accomplish their objectives. Not only do they know what organization is required, but they can mentally design the necessary configuration of resources in terms of quantity, structure, sequence, and output. This is not to say that this skill is always perfectly conceptualized, for adjustments must be made in most instances. However, leaders have a "sixth sense" of how things should work, and they set about the task of amassing resources and forming a framework for integration and interaction.

3. People Selection—A leader must select people to undertake the various assignments necessary to achieve the objectives of a group. Along with all the "human" aspects of leadership, such as traits and qualities, a successful leader will impart to subordinates his or her interest in their personal and professional development. This interest causes subordinates to perceive that leaders are enhancing their development and are growing in their own leadership potential.

4. Directing/Consulting—Leaders are skilled in directing the use of resources (financial, human, property). The directional aspect of their behavior is manifested by making and communicating decisions, instructing subordinates, and managing changes that occur in a dynamic environment. The consultative aspect of their position makes them a resource to others who use them as a sounding board and advice transmitter, as opposed to an instruction transmitter. Some leaders are proportionately unbalanced in their directing/consulting role, which can raise difficulties in the wrong circumstances. However, one does not have to be equally balanced in this regard; the skill is manifested by knowing which part of that role is called for at any given time and with what degree of intensity. Astute leaders also know that subordinates often regard advice and suggestions as direction, and leaders often frame their communications in this manner.

5. Monitoring—Leaders need to be constantly alert as to what is and is not occurring in the arenas in which their organizations operate. Consequently, through observation, research, periodic reports, data analysis, and hypothetical questioning, successful leaders keep their fingers on the pulse of the group. Monitoring skills allow them to shift resources in a manner that adjusts to the environment in order to optimize the organization's position. In monitoring the organization, successful leaders know when to use fingertip control, turn slightly or sharply, accelerate, or slam on the brakes.

6. Measuring—Measurement represents the leadership skill whereby results are evaluated, elements leading to the results are analyzed, and performances are assessed objectively. Leaders establish measurement systems to give them feedback on an organization's level of success not only as it is measured by its own standards but also as it is compared to other organizations in the same environment. Corrective action can be taken as necessary. As measurements become visible, the leadership skill cycle continues to revolve, hopefully in a progressive manner.

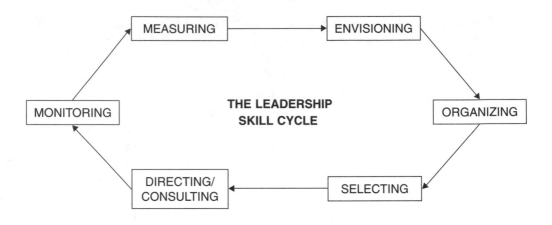

MEASURING → ENVISIONING

MONITORING

**THE LEADERSHIP
SKILL CYCLE**

ORGANIZING

DIRECTING/
CONSULTING ← SELECTING

The Leadership Power Base

Power is a much-used and much-abused word, and many people do not recognize that it is an underlying platform for leadership actions. There are six leadership power bases, none of which are mutually exclusive. Indeed, many leaders combine or attempt to combine several of them in order to synergize their leadership standing.

1. Coercion is the use or threat of physical force and/or mental duress to compel obedience and/or repress activity. At the height of a disagreement, you may have heard a superior say to a subordinate, or vice versa, "Let's go outside and settle this once and for all," as though pure physical dominance would transfer to the organizational relationship. An organizational superior also can exert a Svengalian influence over a subordinate to the degree that the subordinate is a mental slave to the master-superordinate. The forcing of one's will on an another to do something illegal or contrary to policy, for example, is a case of mental coercion. Harassment also falls into this category. Coercion is the rawest form of power and is rarely used by successful leaders.

2. Resource power involves the allocation and interplay of organizational resources from a superordinate to a subordinate. Budget allocations, information flow, office space assignments, bonuses, promotions, and numerous other examples of resources that can be handed out or withheld reflect the use of resource power.

3. Legal power is the most rational and common power base. It provides a vested right by law, charter, or policy to engage in an activity. Most organizations and professions need a certificate or license from a governmental agency that empowers them to operate. At the individual leadership level, the appointment or promotion of a person to the leadership position is the legality that gives the designee the right to function and use resources pertinent to the position. Press releases announcing these appointments are more than recognition courtesies; they alert the world that the designee is the person they must seek out if they need anything from that office.

4. Identification power refers to the charisma or magnetism of an individual that gives that individual influence over others. When someone has the power, others admire and are inspired by it, which causes subordinates or a constituency to do what the charismatic individual wants done. Politicians, athletes, and Hollywood stars often rely heavily on identification for their base of power.

5. Expertise is simply the combination of knowledge and experience applied to a given situation. If one knows what one is doing and others do not, then one possesses expertise power. When a vehicle breaks down, for example, the mechanic who can fix it has the expertise power, regardless of the lofty positions or titles of the passengers.

6. Cultural power varies, depending on the culture and the environment. It is power born of deference to a group or individual based on the customs and mores of that society. Some societies venerate the elderly; some venerate females; and others venerate males or the eldest male or female heir. Power attaches to the members of the group that the culture deems worthy of such influence. A chief in a Native American tribal society is an example of a culturally assigned leadership role.

The Leadership Capstone: Attitude

Now that we have defined and discussed traits, qualities, and skills, all of which are inherent in successful leadership, we need to consider the "capstone" of individual leadership talent: attitude. An attitude is a mental posture a person has that underlies behavior and relationships with other people. It influences how a person regards his or her environment, which can have remarkably positive or negative outcomes. It has often been said that true leaders impact the situation more than they allow the situation to impact them; they manage the moment rather than letting themselves be managed by the moment.

A positive attitude can inspire subordinates and result in a positive environment. Conversely, a negative attitude—which we call "baditude"—can sour subordinates and result in failure.

Let's take a look at the elements of a positive attitude and a negative attitude.

COMPONENTS OF A GOOD ATTITUDE

1. Approachability is apparent in one's spirit, facial expression, demeanor, and personality. It is perceived pleasantness, receptivity to others, and an ease in interacting with people.

2. Respect is reflected in the manner in which one relates to and treats other people. By recognizing the presence, dignity, and values of others, one shows them respect; respect is manifested in courtesy and sincerity.

3. Ethics are reflected in one's behavioral pattern. They are fundamental values that cause others to regard someone as trustworthy and reliable and as exercising good judgment to do the right thing despite the temptation to do otherwise.

4. Cooperation refers to the ability to work with other people as a team to achieve mutually desired goals.

5. Objectivity is the ability to view a situation or address issues nonemotionally so they can be dealt with directly and fairly, without extraneous or personal factors entering into decisions.

6. Effectiveness is the ability to get things done when they should be done and in the manner they need to be done. It is the ability to meet or surpass one's assignment at or above prescribed standards.

7. Efficiency is the economical use of resources, including time, funds, people, and property, that eliminates or minimizes waste. It maximizes the input–output ratio.

8. Discretion is the professional, social, and emotional sensitivity to know when to say something in proper tone and language and when not to say things of an inappropriate nature or at an awkward time.

9. Listening is the ability to give focused attention to what others are saying, free from distraction and mental wandering. It is the intellectual connection to what the speaker is saying, as opposed to hearing, which is the physical act of receiving sound waves.

10. Generosity does not necessarily refer to monetary largess, but it does involve making compliments, making time for people, and volunteering.

11. Empathy is the ability to place oneself in the position of another and to understand, although not necessarily to accept, the perspective of that person. It is intellectual sympathy, not emotional sympathy.

COMPONENTS OF A BAD ATTITUDE (BADITUDE)

1. Self-absorption is the preoccupation with benefiting one's self instead of the group or organization.

2. Sarcasm refers to snide and cynical statements made to deride a plan, a project, or a person.

3. Contentious people approach things with a combative nature. They have a two-dimensional worldview in which one either wins or loses, and they rely on clashes to get their way.

4. Partiality or favoritism, which in its worst form is recognized as prejudice, distorts rational and objective decision making.

5. Laziness is not doing what is supposed to be done or not getting it done in an appropriate and timely manner.

6. Sabotage is the intentional undermining of plans, projects, and people. It also can take a more subtle form in individuals who fail to complete assignments and do not perform at their highest level.

7. Gossip is spreading stories, false or true, that do not serve purposes for constructive advancement of the organization.

8. Hypocrisy is saying one thing and doing another, usually to the detriment of the group.

9. Know-it-alls are impervious to instruction, recommendations, suggestions, and advice. They dismiss these things as unnecessary and irrelevant, and the group suffers the consequences.

10. Volatility is the eruptive nature of an individual that calls that person's stability and reliability into question.

11. Moroseness is the outward manifestation of internal sulking. The sullen demeanor is repelling, discouraging, and, perhaps, fear inducing to others.

Successful leaders know that it is their attitude and fortitude, not necessarily their aptitude or gratitude, that will determine their altitude within their organization.

Types of Groups

A leader, by definition, must have a following, and in the realm of human relationships, followers are groups of people. We need to look at who these groups are, what they are, what characteristics they possess, and how they should be measured, from an organization's viewpoint. It is a simultaneously complex but intriguing subject.

Let's get definitions out of the way first. Recognizing that definitions can vary according to purpose, we realize we need to start from a firm, accepted foundation. A **group** is a collection of two or more persons assembled in order to satisfy a need or desire through an interrelationship. The needs and desires may or may not be the same for each participant, and the intensity of the need and desire may differ. There does not necessarily need to be continuous visual, written, or audible communication, although it is a rare group that does not communicate regularly. The perceived expectation of affiliation of a participant with other group members and the bonding that occurs can give rise to group behavior. This is what separates a group from a set of individuals, a mob, a crowd, or a random audience.

A **formal group** is an assembly of persons brought together for an express purpose known to the participants. Examples are business organizations and school classes. An **informal group** is a meeting of persons for an unspecified purpose, more for the benefit of the participant as an individual than for the achievement of a designated goal. Examples of informal groups include kaffeeklatsches or a pickup lunch-hour bridge or chess game. Informal groups often evolve into formal groups, and formal groups sometimes devolve, in function if not in title, to informal groups.

Groups also can be categorized as voluntary or involuntary. A **voluntary group** is one that can be entered and left freely. Examples are associations and political parties. An **involuntary group** is one in which the ease of entry and departure is limited. The military is an example of an involuntary group. Groups can be **elected**, such as a board of directors; **selected**, such as corporate committees; **occupationally required** by a license, such as lawyers and CPAs; **honorary**, such as medal of honor winners; **exclusive**, such as insurance or real estate million-dollar round tables; or **secretive**, such as a "fifth column." As you see, groups can be categorized over several criteria.

As a leader, you need to consider the profile of the group you are leading. Do not relate to your followers on an individual-by-individual basis only without considering group dynamics. The achievement of your goal will be determined in part by its acceptance by the group. Here are some group characteristics of which you should be conscious in order to have an optimal relationship.

1. Size—Is the group small or large? Small groups usually foster frequent and close communication. Seven or fewer persons usually define a small group. The rule of thumb is that this should also be the maximum number of direct reports a manager (leader) should have in an organization. Eight to 70 persons is generally considered a midsize group, and more than 70 usually is considered a large group.

2. Stratification—Who is assembled? Is it a subgroup of a larger group? Is it everyone in the organization? Department heads? One department? Unit managers? The day shift? Understand that position differences between and among group members can lead to status affirmation ploys by higher-status group members and inhibition on the part of lower-status group members.

3. Homogeneity/heterogeneity—How similar are the demographic characteristics of group members, such as socioeconomic status, age, interests, gender, and work experience? Homogeneous groups usually coalesce faster than heterogeneous groups, for better or for worse. This characteristic raises diversity management issues of which the leader must be aware and which the leader must address as necessary.

4. Familiarity—To what degree is there a mutual acquaintanceship of group members to one another's personal lives and relationships outside the organization? High group familiarity can lead to stronger group ties than leader loyalty. The group is often self-protective when there is high familiarity content and will administer its own sanctions. Group members may not always tell the leader of internal group problems, believing they can work these out among themselves.

5. Efficacy—To what degree is the group operating efficiently as a unit? Groups that work well together could resent any personnel changes. They can freeze new employees out, for example. Rookies at NFL training camps are often razzed as part of the initiation process.

6. Compatibility—To what degree is mutual respect, agreeableness, and visible cooperation evident among group members versus contentiousness, one-upmanship, conflict, and contempt? Open conflict can be dealt with by the leader more easily than group-protected internal hostility.

7. Commitment—What do group members feel towards one another— intense loyalty, benign neutrality, hostility? Strong group identity can lead to immense achievement by the group, and vice versa.

8. Accessibility—With what degree of ease can one be included in the group? Is it open to everyone? Is it an "inner circle"? Is it restricted? Is it by invitation? The higher the standards for group participation, the greater the probability for group achievement.

9. Control—To what degree does the group regulate the behavior of its members? What are group expectations and chastisements for absenteeism, tardiness, inappropriate remarks, or attempts at dominance by a member of a group? A leader is often well advised to let the group administer its own control sanctions rather than to exert his or her own authority.

10. Flexibility—To what degree are the group's activities marked by informal behavior rather than rigid adherence to specific procedures? Casual, directed behavior can often lead to greater sustained group accomplishment than can inflexible, specified behavior.

11. Autonomy—To what degree does one group act independently from other groups? Does it take assignments from other groups or does it determine its own activities? An autonomous group will usually achieve at a higher level than will a dependent group.

12. Participation—What is the level of time and effort constituents devote to the group's activity? Does it extend beyond the assigned time and tasks so that group members volunteer extra effort and time to ensure completion of the group's objective?

Any group, the participants of which are in frequent contact with one another, will develop a group personality that is *different from and more than a composite of* the personalities of its members. A group develops its own persona. The group personality will be both a reflection of and a reaction to the leader. A designated or an appointed leader entering the group's environment must learn to deal with the group personality as well as the personalities of individual members. The challenge is no less daunting for an elected leader, for each constituent wants the elected leader to represent his or her values and positions to the greatest extent possible.

Group dynamics play a major role in leader success. Just think of how many times you have been surprised at the outcome of a meeting, process, or event in which you have been a participant. The outcome was due to group factors at work!

Group Behavior

In the last section we concluded that groups have a personality of their own over and above the individual personalities of group members. Now we will discuss some aspects of group behavior that a leader should know about in order to get the maximum performance out of the group.

1. When first assembled, groups are poised with anticipatory attention.
The dynamics of the first meeting, or the first meeting after a period of time, are crucial to the subsequent performance of the group. The spirit of the group members is generally high, their minds are fresh, and physical fatigue has not set in. Group members are curious about and eager to receive or form their own direction. Many leadership efforts have been lost at a group's inception due to faulty performance in the opening moments. First impressions are semipermanent impressions in a group setting; it is critical that you lead with your strengths when first approaching a group.

2. In a group setting, the notion of "impossibility" is reduced.
Part of the group personality syndrome is to mentally or vocally demean the difficulty or impossibility of an assigned or suggested task. Often this is the result of the bravado of one or more key group members, but just as often it is the reluctance of the group, or any member, to acknowledge a "can't do" attitude. As group members consciously or subconsciously jockey for recognition

and status within the group, a feeling of "I/we can do anything—let's get going" often pervades the group. Just as individuals can exceed apparent human limits on occasion, so can groups. Consequently, group involvement can accelerate individual effort, which, in turn, can result in the group's superior performance. Athletic coaches call this momentum. The requirement is to maintain *perpetual* momentum; the group's adrenalin can aid in this endeavor.

3. Groups foster a sense of diminished personal responsibility.

The larger the group, the greater the chance any individual member can remain anonymous. As a result, the general responsibility for group actions is distributed over the members and shared by them in an equal or predetermined, proportional manner. Thus, no single group member other than the leader has sole responsibility; this could affect the group's judgment. This is why every so often a group will go off "half-cocked," whereas if each of the members had been approached individually, the results might not have been the same.

The leader is ultimately responsible, of course, but when the group is making decisions, the leader is simply the representative or spokesperson, even though the leader may provide direction and channel activity. The elected leader functions primarily as the group's example in such situations. The selected or designated leader is the focal point of decisions, and most group members will not feel a compelling personal responsibility for these decisions since they are "just" participants and not the decision-makers.

4. Unless specifically assigned a reporting responsibility, most group members will not think about the purpose of the group or desired outcomes outside group meetings.

Group members, usually due to the time pressures of their own jobs, will not devote much time to preparing for group meetings. An exception occurs when a group member has a particular point or program he or she wishes to present, but even then the member's attention will be devoted to that aspect rather than to the total overview of the group's functioning. The group perceives the leadership to hold responsibility for coordinating, integrating, and summarizing group direction and activities, and it is correct in this assumption. Consequently, group members will press for issues that are important to them, realizing that other group members and their desires will be a moderating influence. The fundamental principle in group bargaining strategy is to ask for more than you expect to get. Group members know this, and it is one reason they usually accept a leader's judgments that fall short of what they initially ask. When a group member cannot accept the outcome, he or she often severs affiliation with the group.

5. A group setting is conducive to exaggeration.

Exaggeration of benefits of belonging to the group, threats to the group's existence or performance, and praise or criticism of the group will occur informally and spread rapidly. This is due in part to what the group and its participants hear versus what is being said. There is a tendency to amplify the good news or bad news from member to member in cross discussions, as each group member wants others to react with the same degree of understanding and intensity. Usually the loudest, but not necessarily the most rational, voice dominates. You can attain a "fever pitch" faster in a group setting than you can in dealing with individuals on a one-to-one basis.

6. A group setting is conducive to polarized thinking.
Ideas, suggestions, or opinions presented to groups are usually accepted or rejected in totality rather than analyzed for positive and negative elements. A large group is an excellent base for criticism, but it is less conducive to creative implementation, except in the instance of brainstorming sessions. Most group members will recognize extreme positions or ideas; some group members will differentiate and place themselves in between the two poles, making it difficult to find the exact solution acceptable to these members. Consequently, many decisions coming from a group represent the "least detrimental" rather than the "most far-reaching" position. A leader has to consider these facts and act in a manner that will result in the best long-term interest of the organization and constituency.

7. Contagion is rapidly and easily accomplished in a group setting.
Groups are given to more impulsive behavior than that of the average individual. They have a greater impetus to transform suggestions into action and demand immediate achievement. This is due in part to the stimulation each participant enjoys as the result of being a group member and the tendency to act emotionally which stems from being in an interpersonal setting. Frequently, this desire for action manifests itself in the demand for appointment of subcommittees, because most group members recognize the limitations of large groups.

8. A group will structure itself with respect to the roles participants play.
As group members become familiar with one another through communication interchanges, they will establish their own niches in group activity. For example, one participant frequently will remind others of the basic objectives of the group in analyzing the current discussions or activity in order to maintain focus on those objectives. Most every group has, and needs, a person who provides comic relief. Someone will act informally as parliamentarian if a formal designation has not been made. Other participants will settle into their own roles. Once individual members have developed their roles, they may have difficulty changing them. If they attempt to change, other group members may meet initial efforts with chastisement, as change represents a disrupting impact on existing group dynamics.

9. Groups rely heavily on symbols.
Recognizing that people are more transitory than institutions, and desiring an allegiance to an impersonal representation of the group rather than blind

loyalty to a leader, symbolism plays a major role in solidifying the group. The use of symbols and slogans, as part of the culture of the group, can transcend differences among individuals and act as a unifying element for the total group. Symbols visually represent the higher purpose for which the group exists and can be helpful in preventing fractionalization. An organization's logo and flag are examples of such need-fulfilling symbols.

Group effectiveness usually falls between the maximum possible and the minimum allowable. The result rests with the leadership, who must use group dynamics to achieve what is best achieved in a group setting. Sometimes it is better not to assemble a group. Other times it is better to advise individuals as to what you want accomplished prior to group assembly or to meet with individuals one at a time. These alternatives are more time consuming, but they allow the leader more direct control over the situation.

The Environment

Now that we have discussed several aspects of leaders and groups, we must turn our attention to an equally ambiguous element of the leadership dynamic, the environment. Leadership characteristics are bound by the personality and the range of talent and flexibility of the person occupying the leadership position, and the group character tends to change only as the leadership changes or individual members enter and leave the setting. The environment, however, is highly volatile, fluid, and fleeting. In fact, the situation is never static; it is perpetually changing, because it encompasses both external and internal factors. Still, environments can be analyzed and categorized, and it behooves the leader to approach *all* situations as being leadable.

One must first consider factors over which the organization has virtually little or no control. Such factors include an abrupt change in the world or national economy, the issuance of a new governmental regulation, resource scarcity such as utility crunches, the appearance of a competitor in the same market area, natural disasters, and so on. There are some external factors, however, over which the organization can exert some control. These include community involvement activities; having employees run for local office; and sponsorship of local, regional, or national events that invite good public exposure. Engaging in these activities is known as being "proactive."

Internally, events also can occur over which the organization has little or no control. Examples of these events include heavy employee absence due to illness or destruction of company assets due to a calamity such as a flood or fire. Finally, the internal environment can change because of factors that are generated internally. Examples of these changes would be decisions to enter a new market area, expand the product or service line, change human resource policies, or acquire or divest divisions or subsidiaries. We can set up a matrix of possibilities to categorize the four different types of environments.

ENVIRONMENT

	External	Internal
1.	Stable	Stable
2.	Stable	Unstable
3.	Unstable	Stable
4.	Unstable	Unstable

1. Stable-Stable Environment—represents the most desired state and is what most people mean when they say "business as usual." External and internal elements are predictable, and a slight change on one side of the environment is balanced quickly and accurately by adaptation on the other side. Changes that do occur are planned or forecast, and there are no big waves in the organizational waters. A state of flux always exists, of course. That is why leaders have daily and hourly reports. Generally speaking, however, the systems employed by an organization are working, and an atmosphere of relative calm and normalcy prevails. Harsh authoritarian and autocratic methods will meet with spoken or unspoken employee rejection. A solicitous or nonexcitable approach by management is expected and is usually appreciated.

2. Stable-Unstable Environment—is the next easiest situation to lead, because the focus can be on the internal instability with normal attention being given externally until the internal situation is remedied. Depending on the nature of the internal instability, management can activate a contingency plan. Many matters of internal instability in an organization reside in the personnel area and can be overcome by promotion, transfer, reorganization, overtime, temporary hiring, termination, use of consultants, or change of personnel policies. In such circumstances, the leader must, and is expected to, act quickly and forcefully. A leader needs to preplan. Decisive action carried out quickly and efficiently can reinforce the charisma and reputation of the leader.

3. Unstable-Stable Environment—represents a frustrating leadership problem in that instability in the external environment is largely perceived as being beyond the influence and control of the leader. The singular benefit is that the internal organizational environment is relatively stable, allowing for primary focus on the outside. In this situation many leaders mentally if not physically operate under the "I can't do anything about it" syndrome. The true leader, however, rises to the occasion and guides the organization through the stormy waters of unpredictability. To do this, the leader must communicate completely and efficiently with subordinates and outside sources so that the assessment of the environment can be kept current. Decision making in an unpredictable environment is hazardous at best and catastrophic at worst. Sometimes the best decision under such conditions is to do nothing different until the situation clears up. The world cannot stand incessant unpredictability, and consequently the external environment will settle down after a relatively short time, although some irreversible changes may have taken place. On the other hand, one cannot be immobilized, and the leader must be able to recognize when it is necessary to act.

4. **Unstable-Unstable Environment**—represents the worst-case situation and often stems from the cause-and-effect relationship between the external environment and the organization. Bankruptcies and dissolutions are often the results of such an environment. In this situation, leadership attention must be fairly equally divided between the inside and outside environments, as changes in one area will necessitate a balancing action in the other. Such circumstances take the greatest financial and human toll, but they also create the greatest satisfactions. The external environment is likely to settle first. This situation often results in the mental and often physical resignation of management. The leader is tested in this unstable environment; how he or she acts is the ultimate measure of leadership.

Leadership Foundations

Having discussed several aspects of the leader as a person, the group that is being lead, and environmental characteristics, we now need to integrate all of these components into scenarios in which a leader must perform. We must start with leadership foundations.

One of the finest compliments you can give to a person in organizational life is that "he/she is a leader." We have identified nine elements that we believe are the foundations of perceived and/or actual leadership.

1. **Bearing**—Bearing refers to body carriage, presence, and physical demeanor. A confident walk, alertness, an air of command and determination, a perceived buoyancy of spirit, and a positive attitude connote a strong impression of being in control. A stooped, baffled, hangdog, and fatigued appearance inspires and motivates no one.

2. **Countenance**—This is the facial counterpart of bearing. A person's expression shows his or her mental and emotional state. Alert eyes, a pleasant visage, a quickness to smile, and a calm presence present an inviting aura.

3. Self-control—Leaders never lose control of themselves, mentally or physically, under any circumstances. They also know that anything can be managed, and they employ their experience and talents skillfully, based on sound principles and a high level of competence. They do not fly off the handle, engage in tirades, become emotional, or shrink from adversity. They are strong in their enthusiasm and their restraint.

4. Communication Skills—An articulate mind empowers articulate speech, and a cultivated mind empowers cultivated writing. Leaders have the ability to speak and write clearly and incisively, measuring their words carefully and using tone and pace befitting the occasion. They do not overtalk or undercommunicate, or use language as a weapon; they use language as a tool to convey their thoughts.

5. Thirst for Knowledge—Leaders read voraciously, are inquisitive, explore all avenues of their responsibilities, and constantly seek opportunities to increase their understanding. They do not sit on their laurels, slide into a mentality of "it's good enough," or allow themselves to become outdated or intellectually slothful.

6. Integrity—Leaders adhere to the highest of standards, both personally and professionally. They are people who keep their word, follow up, abide by a moral compass, and are known and admired for their honesty, rectitude, and strong character. They possess a reputation of being honorable and responsible.

7. Strong Qualifications—Leaders have a proven track record of involvement, success, and accomplishment. While their formal resumes list the history of their attainments, their prominence is such that they do not need to brandish it. They are known by reputation as leaders, experts, and visionaries.

8. Good Judgment—Given their general and specific competence, acumen, and experience, leaders are looked to for insightful judgment of situations, proposals, and projects. Although not infallible, they can observe things quickly, make assessments, and instinctively and rapidly calculate what is needed to be successful. They are stable, objective thinkers, and they readily acknowledge the positives and negatives of any situation. They do not sugarcoat problems or difficulties, nor do they let the excitement of the challenge and enthusiasm dilute their analysis and critical approach.

9. People Skills—Leaders relate well to others and are open, cordial, courteous, and responsive. They possess empathy and are active, interested, sincere listeners, giving individuals their undivided attention. They are never discourteous and never lose their poise, composure, or respect for others.

L eadership Character

There are numerous definitions of the word "character," but the one on which we are focusing here is "the essential quality and pattern of behavior found in one's moral constitution." If personality and reputation emerge from the strong character of a leader, it becomes important to identify the elements of character so others can adopt or develop these traits as part of their own growth processes. The presence and combination of the following seven character elements can result in a highly effective and successful leader.

1. Authority is bimodal. *Personal* authority can be displayed in demeanor, presence, body carriage, manner of speaking, personal charisma, interactions with others, and types of reactions. A self-controlled, self-paced, strong aura is derived from self-confidence and past experience. *Professional or organizational* authority allows one to use and allocate resources commensurate with the position one holds. This is conferred authority and is manifest as the result of a promotion, election, selection, or appointment.

An effective leader needs to utilize both types of authority. One without the other is not nearly as good as having sufficient quantities of both.

2. Decisiveness is the ability to make decisions in a timely, objective, and thoughtful manner. It does not refer to rash reaction, rigid inflexibility, or quick pronouncement. It embraces focused determination and clarity with a resolve to reach identified goals. It embraces a sense of decisiveness as part of a dynamic process, and it is the forerunner of action.

3. Inspiration is an intangible character element that motivates others to raise their efforts well beyond their normal level. This is possible if employees are intellectually and emotionally instilled with the rightness of their activity.

A number of leaders are able to inspire others for a short period of time or to inspire others when they are physically present. The most effective leaders, however, are able to inspire others over a sustained period of time without being physically present.

4. Integrity refers to a worthiness of self. It allows people to rely on a leader's word and assures that the leader will always act morally and ethically. Integrity is not piety, nor is it sanctimony. Integrity is absolute, not relative. Anything less than total integrity constitutes some measure of dishonesty.

5. Empathy allows an effective leader to be able to see things from another person's perspective. Equally important is the ability to communicate an understanding of the other person's position and perspective, even though one may not agree with that person. Empathy is the second step in any successful negotiating process. (The first step is to recognize the differing position.) Empathy does not necessarily connote passion, sentimentality, or acquiescence.

6. Receptive leaders display openness to people, ideas, and change. Receptivity involves being approachable, listening intently, not allowing preconceived notions to block communication, and respecting the dignity of others. Receptivity is not passivity, nor is it automatic acceptance. It embraces sensitivity and sensibility coupled with the desire to grow (both personally and organizationally) through an openness to new opportunities and/or refinements to existing opportunities. It is signaled by a smile, eye contact, a courteous tone, and relevant body language.

7. Vigor conveys spirit, movement, activity, and an unyielding quest for progress that is evident to all who surround you. It includes forward motion, resiliency, an upbeat attitude, drive, and determination. Vigor does not convey hyperactivity for the sake of activity or a "make work" or "all-talk-and-no-action" philosophy. Vigor is both mental and physical; it is steady and perpetual.

The Roles of Leaders

We are perpetually impressed and amazed at the ability of leaders to function with effectiveness and efficiency in light of the multiple demands made on them. They are truly extraordinary people, able to shift instantaneously from one role to another without losing momentum or hesitating in thought or action.

People are different, and top leaders are uncommonly different. To some degree, the head of any self-contained organizational unit functions as the leader of that unit (or at least the position holder), and many midlevel managers experience the same demands the overall leader faces on daily basis. Accordingly, many of the following roles also apply to these lower-level leaders.

1. Creator of Standards, Values, and Organizational Culture.
The leader needs to establish and maintain standards, both by personal example and organizational fiat. However, personal example carries more weight. Standards are required for every element of the operating system and every component of organizational activity. The leader is the author and projector of organizational values, embracing such issues as quality, customer orientation, and demonstrated concern for social responsibility as well as financial accountability. The leader is the personification of the overall organizational culture. The leader, in every sense of the word, is the human essence of the enterprise and the people who comprise it.

2. Risk Taker/Risk Maker.

The leader is ultimately responsible for that which he or she makes happen within the enterprise. Setting of new directions; entering uncharted waters; making critical personnel, marketing, financial, and public affairs decisions, and fine-tuning current operations all carry a risk element. The success or failure of these endeavors eventually will be laid at the feet of the leader. The leader is a risk maker as well, challenging conventional ideas with creative concepts, inspiring subordinates to reach beyond their current grasp, and establishing conditions where major breakthroughs can occur against the odds. The leader must do so, however, in an environment where there is not fear but an abhorrence of failure.

3. Chief Tactician.

The leader needs to deal with the short-term future as well as the longer-range perspective. He or she has to look at the annual operating plan, quarterly reports, monthly results, and flash indices. Rapid responses must be made to competitive attacks, the vagaries of public sentiment, and the fluctuation of financial markets.

4. Chief Strategist.

The longer-term outlook also occupies the leader's attention, for he or she must be both far- and nearsighted for the enterprise to grow and prosper throughout the years. Leaders look for lasting achievements, recognizing that while they and their positions within the organization may be transitory, the organization itself must endure and stand the test of time.

5. Chief Spokesperson.

The leader is the cumulative personality of the organization to both the outside and inside worlds. At major positive or negative critical points, the leader must stand before the world and clearly state the position of the organization relative to the matters at hand. Both mental and verbal articulation are required, as is an ability to synethize disparate functions and/or events into a cohesive whole so that the organization is positioned in the most favorable posture possible.

6. Chief Negotiator.

An organization is a system of interacting components, and, as such, friction and conflicts occur with some degree of regularity. The leader is the chief negotiator among the components: an arbitrator managing the friction and hurdling the conflicts in the best long-term interest of the enterprise. The leader is often the moderator between and among competing concepts, approaches, and personalities within the organization and should be a stabilizing countenance.

7. Chief Observer.

The leader must know the anatomy of the environments and the economy in which operations are conducted, so that his or her practiced eye can catch the slightest change and determine whether or not such change is fleeting or fundamental.

8. Buck Stopper.
The leader represents that person in an organization beyond whom decisions do not pass without a final determination. The leader has the last word.

hat Sets Leaders Apart

Within any grouping of people, be it a city, a company, a team, a social club, or an association, a structure will emerge that establishes a position of leadership. The person who occupies that position gets there through election, selection, appointment, inheritance, or seniority. Although this is the usual order of things, there can be exceptions. Nevertheless, it behooves us to examine and analyze what sets leaders apart from others.

1. Leaders are both proactive and reactive.
Leaders get themselves—and others—moving, and when course corrections are called for due to changing conditions or surprise elements, they can adapt immediately and adeptly. They have a high energy level and focused foresight. They know where they want the group to be at a given point in time and strive for that position. Leaders do not let obstructions or delays discourage them; instead, they forge ahead undaunted in pursuit of their goals.

2. Leaders possess charisma.
Sometimes this charisma is borne of the physical presence of the individual; other times it comes from the individual's personality. Usually, however, it is a mixture of these qualities and more. Charisma can be cultivated, and strong leaders can maintain their charismatic nature.

3. Leaders empower others.
Empowerment goes beyond delegation of authority. It embraces inspiration, motivation, passion, trust, expectations, and action. Leaders are comfortable with empowerment because they have a fundamental respect for people. When, on occasion, they experience disappointment, they regard it as a temporary aberration rather than a generalized deterioration of the system. Leaders recognize that while individuals may have some faults, they may also be stirred to achieve at higher levels. Leaders focus on accomplishment.

4. Leaders attract and marshal resources.
Leaders are able to draw resources to them that allow movement to occur. Leaders are usually compellingly persuasive in advancing toward an envisioned goal.

5. Leaders are optimistic and creative.

Leaders overcome challenges and hurdles through innovative thought, unconventional approaches, tenaciousness, and positive reinforcement. They exude a positive attitude and spirit, a receptive persona, and an in-command demeanor. They are not overwhelmed or immobilized by events, rebuffed by roadblocks, or dispirited by naysayers. Leaders have a buoyant attitude and a lively imagination, and they have the ability to turn a small idea into a larger concept, acting as catalysts for action.

6. Leaders are team members.

Leaders recognize that although they are ultimately responsible for their areas, they are also one component of a larger whole. They are participative rather than aloof; personable rather than mean spirited; conscientious rather than unconscionable; and focused on the group rather than self-absorbed. Leaders do not regard themselves as better than the group; they accept and care about their roles and responsibilities.

7. Leaders are exemplars.

Leaders know that they represent their organizations. Accordingly, they are ever mindful of professionalism, self-discipline, decorum, and the desire for improvement. Leaders know that success is not an individual achievement. Rather, it is a result of synchronized efforts in which the individuals of a group must collaborate. Leaders take satisfaction in accomplishment, not adulation.

Leaders Are Not Bureaucrats

People in leadership positions usually have a style, charisma, persona, or personality that causes others to follow their lead in achieving their goals. Bureaucrats, those who are in responsible positions but do not seize leadership opportunities, have a style, demeanor, or manner that causes others to be unsure about their ability to lead. When this occurs, results are less than could be possible. Bureaucrats are position holders; leaders are position growers.

On occasion, organizations, departments, and teams fail miserably due to the "bureaucratic mindset." Some contrasts between leaders and bureaucrats in terms of their styles and attitudes follow:

- Leaders say, "We can do it." *Bureaucrats say. "We can try it."*

- Leaders look for continued progress. *Bureaucrats continue to maintain the status quo.*

- Leaders possess and evoke an attitude of improvement. *Bureaucrats are self-satisfied.*

- Leaders play a good game. *Bureaucrats talk a good game.*
- Leaders judge themselves. *Bureaucrats hope others will judge them favorably.*
- Leaders know they must confront problems. *Bureaucrats hope problems will go away.*
- Leaders demand flawless administration. *Bureaucrats get bogged down in administrative detail.*
- Leaders delegate duties and tasks. *Bureaucrats absorb duties and tasks.*
- Leaders are comfortable with their subordinates. *Bureaucrats are comfortable in their offices.*
- A leader says, "I'm responsible." *A bureaucrat says, "It's not my fault."*
- A leader can laugh at himself or herself. *A bureaucrat is offended by bureaucracy-directed humor.*
- A leader shares credit. *A bureaucrat wants all the credit.*
- A leader says, "I'll take the blame." *A bureaucrat says, "Who's to blame?"*
- The leader is a tireless worker. *The bureaucrat is a tired worker.*
- When things get tough, the leader is overwhelming. *When things get tough, the bureaucrat is overwhelmed.*
- The leader goes for the win. *The bureaucrat goes for the tie.*
- The leader is outgoing. *The bureaucrat likes going out.*
- Leaders develop subordinates. *Bureaucrats assign subordinates.*
- The leader is often the team's most valuable player. *The bureaucrat is often the team's most voluble player.*
- Leaders say, "We can fix that." *Bureaucrats say, "I told you it wouldn't work."*
- Leaders are customer oriented. *Bureaucrats are process oriented.*
- Leaders provide direction. *Bureaucrats give instructions.*
- Leaders can manage many things at once. *Bureaucrats prefer to manage one thing at a time.*
- Leaders handle the media effectively. *Bureaucrats allow the media to handle them.*
- Leaders earn respect. *Bureaucrats demand respect.*
- Leaders seek organizational commitment and loyalty. *Bureaucrats require personal commitment and loyalty.*
- Leaders trust key subordinates. *Bureaucrats rely on control systems.*
- Leaders recruit the best talent available. *Bureaucrats do not want to be challenged by subordinates.*

- Leaders teach. *Bureaucrats pontificate.*
- Leaders emphasize standards. *Bureaucrats emphasize discipline.*
- Leaders focus. *Bureaucrats view.*
- Leaders inspire. *Bureaucrats perspire.*
- Leaders manage stress in their lives. *Bureaucrats are managed by stress in their lives.*
- Leaders communicate articulately. *Bureaucrats communicate artfully.*
- Leaders lead for the future. *Bureaucrats let the future take care of itself.*
- Leaders take action at the appropriate time. *Bureaucrats want more advice.*
- Leaders say, "We succeeded in spite of the obstacles." *Bureaucrats say, "We could have succeeded if it weren't for the obstacles."*
- Leaders take advantage of the rules. *Bureaucrats go strictly by the rules.*
- Leaders see the glass as half full. *Bureaucrats do not see the glass.*
- Leaders are generous with their time. *Bureaucrats are protective of their time.*
- When things look as if they are going wrong, leaders cry, "Charge!" *When things look as if they are going wrong, bureaucrats cry, "Foul!"*
- Leaders are gracious. *Bureaucrats are ingratiating.*
- Leaders are aggressive. *Bureaucrats are intrusive.*
- Leaders think strategically. *Bureaucrats think about time off.*
- Leaders are objective. *Bureaucrats are subjective.*
- Leaders enjoy their time. *Bureaucrats put in their time.*
- Leaders lead. *Bureaucrats watch.*

hat Leaders Know

It is often difficult to define or describe what constitutes a leader; however, leaders hold certain values that should be considered and recognized.

- *Leaders* know things can be done, and they do them.
- *Leaders* know that the measure of a team is not how well the team performs when things are going as planned, but how well the team performs when things are not going as planned.
- *Leaders* know that the most important investment they will ever make is in their integrity.

- *Leaders* know that the most important asset they will ever own is their reputation.
- *Leaders* know that the most important expenditure they will ever make is in service to others (the servant leader).
- *Leaders* know that that most important thing they put on in the morning is their smile.
- *Leaders* know that when they are faced with a choice between intelligence and experience, they will chose experience. With intelligence you often get arrogance; with experience you usually get wisdom.
- *Leaders* live their lives through a zoom lens not through a rearview mirror.
- *Leaders* know that small minds talk about people, great minds talk about ideas.
- *Leaders* realize that when they become comfortable, they become vulnerable.
- *Leaders* possess a lot of WIT: Whatever It Takes.
- *Leaders* know that self-confidence comes from internal mastery. Effectiveness comes from external mastery.
- *Leaders* do not let bad experiences make them bitter; they know it makes them better.
- *Leaders* know that life is not to be measured in terms of an "unbeaten season." They know that there will be times when they may lose, but they will never allow themselves to be defeated.
- *Leaders* know that vision involves insight and foresight.
- *Leaders* know that, irrespective of titles, they are CEOs: Competent, Effective, and Organized.
- *Leaders* do not tolerate mediocrity; they know mediocrity is a step toward failure.
- *Leaders* know that maintaining an attitude that works toward improvement requires daily effort.
- *Leaders* realize that success is not an individual achievement. Many people, including subordinates, customers, teachers, mentors, and coaches, participate in it.
- *Leaders* know there is a difference between dictatorship and directorship. The former rests on power; the latter on conferred authority.
- *Leaders* impact situations more than they allow situations to impact them.
- *Leaders* know they should listen twice as much as they talk.

- *Leaders* know there is a difference between positionship and leadership. The former is a location in an organizational structure; the latter is a perception in the minds of a constituency.

- *Leaders* know there is a difference between being exceptional and being an exception. The former is usually accompanied by admiration; the latter is usually accompanied by skepticism.

The Culmination of Individual L.E.A.D.E.R.S.H.I.P.

As we have seen, leadership carries a fascination and attraction for most people. We all like to think we have at least some leadership qualities, and we strive to develop them. We seek to identify which traits, qualities, characteristics, and skills leaders possess so that we can emulate them. The constant fundamental question remains, however, "What results in successful leadership?" At least part of that answer can be found within the word itself. It is the culmination of our discussion on individual leadership.

Loyalty. Leadership is founded on a loyalty quadrant: loyalty to one's organization and its mission, loyalty to organizational superiors, loyalty to subordinates, and loyalty to oneself. Loyalty is multidirectional, moving downward and upward in the organization. When everyone practices it, "loyalty bonds'" occur which produce high morale. Loyalty to oneself is based on maintaining a healthy body, mind, and spirit so that one is always riding the top of the wave in service to others.

Excellence. Leaders know that excellence is a value not an object; they strive for both excellence and success. Excellence is the measurement you make of yourself in assessing what you do and how you do it; success is the external perception others have of you as a leader.

Assertiveness. Leaders possess a mental and physical intensity that causes them to seek control, take command, and focus on the objective(s). Leaders do not show self-doubt, because they are comfortable that they are doing what is right. This, in turn, gives them the courage to take action.

Dedication. Leaders are dedicated to their organization and to achievement. They are action oriented, not passive, and prefer purposeful activity to the status quo. They possess charisma that sets them apart from others, but they are always working in the best interest of their organization.

Enthusiasm. Leaders are the best cheerleaders for their organization and their people. They exude enthusiasm and instill it in others. They possess poise, stability, clear vision, and articulate speech.

Risk Management. Leaders realize risk taking is part of their leadership position. They manage risk rather that letting it manage them, knowing that there are no guaranteed outcomes, no foregone conclusions, and no predestined results. Nonetheless, they measure risk, control it, adapt to it, and surmount it.

Strength. Leaders possess an inner reserve of stamina, fortitude, and vibrancy that gives them a mental toughness, causing them to withstand interruptions, crises, and unforeseen circumstances that would slow down or immobilize most people. Leaders become all the more energized in the face of surprises.

Honor. Leaders understand they will leave a legacy, be it good, bad, or indifferent. True leaders recognize that all their actions and relationships are based on the highest standards of honor and integrity. They do the right things correctly, shun short-term, improper expediency, and set an example for others.

Inspiration. Leaders do not exist without followers. People will follow leaders who inspire them to reach beyond the normal and ordinary to new levels of accomplishment, new heights of well-being, and new platforms of individual, organizational, and societal good. Inspiration is what distinguishes a leader from a position holder; the leader can touch the minds, hearts, and souls of others.

Performance. At the end of the day, leaders rise or fall based on the most critical of all measurements, their performance. Results come first, but the way in which the results are achieved is also critical to sustaining a leader's role. Many "dictators" do not last despite results and many "charismatics" do not last despite personal charm.

Part II

Leadership:
The Life Cycle

■ ■ ■ ■ ■ ■ ■ ■ ■ ■ ■

We now turn our attention to Part II of *Four-Dimensional Leadership*, The Life Cycle. We have created a taxonomy of organizations in their various stages of life and compared it with human development. We take this approach because we are convinced that the leader's qualities, values, and skills must be congruent with needs of the organization at its life-cycle stage in order for the organization to advance.

The absence of leadership creates anxiety and decay. The presence of leadership creates confidence and spirit.

Christopher C. Muller, Ph.D.

If you want to develop the virtues and qualities to be a leader, behave as though you already possess them.

William P. Fisher, Ph.D.

The Organization

As we have noted, an organization is a group of people brought together to achieve an objective. The group members, including the leader, usually have a title or a rank that indicates their place in the organization. This structure is most commonly depicted in an organization chart, a diagram displaying the arrangement of the organization's divisions, departments, and offices, and their relationships to one another.

An organization is not a building, institution, chart, or edifice. Like people, organizations have life cycles which can be both characterized and analyzed to provide a portrait of an organization at any given time. We will use a corporate entity as an example in our discussion, because that is a prevailing framework for many organizations operating around the world.

We will match the attributes of individual leader(s) with the organization's stage of life-cycle development. If individual leadership attributes coincide with organizational developmental needs at the given moment in time, there can be a synergistic impact that results in success. Were there to be a mismatch of individual leadership talent and the organizational stage of development, an incompatibility will exist that usually proves irreconcilable. If this happens, the organization either remains at the status quo or dissolves, and the leader (CEO) usually departs, voluntarily or otherwise.

We identify six life-cycle stages. The business stage is listed to the left, the concept stage appears in the middle, and the leadership role is listed on the right.

Business Life Cycle	Concept Life Cycle	Leadership Role
1. Creation	Conception/Gestation	Entrepreneur
2. Construction	Survival	Implementer
3. Development	Growth	Navigator
4. Expansion	Experience	Accelerator
5. Cultivation	Maturity	Harvester
6. Renewal*	Legacy/Decline	Explorer**

*At this stage the organization must look for new opportunities to initiate the life-cycle process again. Failing to do so will result in the disappearance of the organization, or at least a passivity that renders it mediocre and ineffective.

**Given that concept life is finite, it is at this stage that leaders become statespersons (often chair of the board without the CEO title, which is usually granted to the president of the organization). Many of these people remain actively engaged in scouting out and exploring new opportunities for the entity. Others, perhaps coincident with a more conservative and cautious life style in general, vegetate in their role. This can lead to organizational decline and eventual failure.

We will discuss each life-cycle stage in turn and suggest the individual leadership attributes required for that phase in the cycle. Moreover, we will identify the primary vulnerabilities that exist at each stage, which can emasculate an organization unless dealt with quickly and forcefully. Tables 2–1 and 2–2 present a visual display of the Organizational Leadership Life-Cycle Paradigm.

S tage I—Creation (Conception/Gestation)

LEADERSHIP ROLE: ENTREPRENEUR

Organizations sprout from an idea or a series of related ideas. One may call such an idea a "vision," a "calling," an "inspiration," or a "notion." The idea may appear in the form of a dream (literally), a desire, an observation of an issue that is not being addressed or could be better addressed, new applications, inventions, or serendipity.

This person, whether called an intrapreneur, entrepreneur, enterpriser, or inventor, takes the idea and begins to shape it within a social, economic, and material resource framework to develop it more fully. It is not unusual for the idea generator to talk to others about the idea; to receive views, suggestions, and advice; and to continue to ruminate on it before reaching a more clearly defined and refined projection of what the idea will accomplish.

At this point, the now well-shaped idea needs to be converted into an actionable form. When a new, innovative concept is conceived, it is common for two or more people to partner to bring it forward to reality. This arrangement is often necessary, as one partner has essential abilities such as financial, administrative, and marketing skills, while another person possesses creative, operational, and mechanical/technical skills. A complementary balance of attributes is, indeed, helpful.

From a corporate perspective, once the concept has been clearly focused, it needs to be seeded and nurtured with financial support, marketing assistance, site and property identification and selection, human resource skill set identification, recruitment, selection, and acculturation. This is what we respectfully term the creation/gestation period, in which everything needs to be ready, in order, and timely for concept realization to occur.

The required leadership attributes at this initial stage, whether residing in one person or shared with others, are entrepreneurial in nature. The prominent and dominant characteristics of Stage I follow.

STAGE I LEADERSHIP ATTRIBUTES

Passion—Passion refers to a fervent optimism for success, being impervious to naysayers and doubters, and having a strong sense and image of enthusiasm and excitement that is easily perceived by different constituencies. The leader exudes a contagious enthusiasm.

Table 2–1 The Organizational Life Cycle: Leadership Attributes and Vulnerabilities

Organization Stage	Creation	Construction	Development	Expansion	Cultivation	Renewal
Leadership Stage	Entrepreneur	Implementer	Navigator	Accelerator	Harvester	Explorer
Primary Attributes	Passion Focus Confidence Stability Motivation Tenacity Energy	Communication Determination Quality mindedness Problem-solving	Planning Administration Relationship Building Educating	Delegation Forcefulness Pragmatism Achiever	Competitiveness Consistency Charisma Character	Opportunist Inquisitive Researcher Ambassador
Life-Cycle Stage	I	II	III	IV	V	VI
Primary Vulnerabilities	Distraction Discouragement Dilution	Undercapitalization Shoddiness Lack of standards Lack of training	Self-satisfaction Overconfidence Personnel Paralysis	Profligacy Overreaching Inflexibility Defections	Entropy Erosion Egotism	Risk aversion Carelessness Vegetation

Table 2–2 The Organizational Leadership Life Cycle

Organization Stage	Creation	Construction	Development	Expansion	Cultivation	Renewal
Leadership Stage	Entrepreneur	Implementer	Navigator	Accelerator	Harvester	Explorer
Concept Stage	Conception/Gestation	Survival	Growth	Experience	Maturity	Legacy Decline
Life-Cycle Stage	I	II	III	IV	V	VI

Focus—Being focused means riveting one's attention to the immediate creation objective and not being distracted by clutter, noise, and the rumors that always populate the marketplace. There is focused insight and foresight.

Confidence—This is a mental and physical demeanor that expresses an air of knowledge. It includes a "can-do" body posture and professional bearing to overcome unexpected events and the criticism of others.

Stability—Stability refers to the quality of living a balanced personal and professional life and not lapsing into uncontrolled anger, irrationality, or excessive celebration. It is the ability to keep a rein on emotions coupled with a sense of reality. Equilibrium is key. Hyperenthusiasm can be counterproductive, as others may regard the leader as delusionary, which causes credibility deterioration.

Motivation—Motivation requires helping constituents such as employees, customers, and suppliers to act in manners appropriate to their roles with the organization through personal demeanor and organizational structure. It also includes radiating positive experiences and enhancing the organizational reputation. Motivation is leader-led momentum that is intellectually transferred.

Tenacity—Tenacity refers to the mental toughness of the inventor/entrepreneur leader, who persists in searching for solutions and realizations despite earlier unsuccessful attempts. Tenacity is one's mental resolution to remain on the course one has set.

Energy—A high level of intensity is essential for leaders to surmount the inevitable hurdles that appear. As a start-up business embraces numerous stimuli, demands, exceptions, expectations, surprises, and upsets, the leader must work tirelessly. Successful leaders often require less sleep than the average person, because their idea-generation mindset races at a rate similar to that of their physical metabolism.

STAGE I PRIMARY VULNERABILITIES

Certainly, the lack of an attribute can be termed a vulnerability, and the absence of any of the aforementioned attributes in Stage I increases the difficulty of progressing through this stage. In addition, however, there are three primary vulnerabilities that may arise, which lead to the catapulting of otherwise good/workable ideas into the trash heap of unfulfilled dreams. The entrepreneurial leader needs to be wary of:

Distraction—An entrepreneur who is derailed from the core substance of the invention or innovation can lose focus and proceed in a direction different from the original concept. There is usually great pressure in the marketplace for conformity (versus creativity) because conformity represents little if any disruption, which the marketplace is happy to avoid. The marketplace does not necessarily enjoy change. The entrepreneurial leader must withstand distractions and maintain focus on the concept.

Discouragement—If one is easily discouraged by a fear of risk-taking, by the perceived amount of resources necessary to move forward, by criticism, or by personal factors, progress becomes half-hearted and can eventually expire. The proverb "hindsight is better than foresight" is certainly true, for many would-be entrepreneurs have had regrets in retrospect that they did not proceed when opportunities presented themselves. The entrepreneurial leader needs courage.

Dilution—Many idea generators look for entrepreneurial support and guidance to help them create their ideas. Indeed, both amateur and professional organizations exist that suggest they can shepherd one's ideas. While this guidance is sometimes a good or necessary step, as in patent applications or copyright submissions, for example, it can also backfire by diluting the original concept to a point of nonrecognition. Many an author has pulled a manuscript out of the hands of the Hollywood producer who would not remain true to the author's original work. There is a fine line between idea refinement and idea dilution. The entrepreneurial leader needs to be able to distinguish one from the other.

If the organization possesses the right type of leadership, and if it overcomes or deftly manages its vulnerabilities, then the organization reaches Stage II.

S tage II—Construction (Survival)

LEADERSHIP ROLE: IMPLEMENTER

At this point, the idea has germinated, and the organization has been born. The appearance of an organization must be followed by close monitoring to insure its viability and sustainability.

New to its environment, the organization must be adeptly aware of conditions so it can ward off threats to its existence, take progressive steps to acclimate within its realm, attract allies, and get "health shots," such as loans, market studies, and employee surveys to prevent early "diseases" from becoming afflictions or fatal infirmities.

The primary focus is survival, which is accomplished by insuring compliance with adopted operating procedures, by paying close attention to internal and external elements impacting on the organization, by short-term planning, and by altering prior plans according to conditions. Major short-falls, mistakes, voids, and shortcomings must be avoided. Otherwise, failure is a definite possibility.

In order to succeed, all of the leadership attributes required in Stage I need to be evident in Stage II. Additionally, the implementer will need the following attributes to succeed.

STAGE II LEADERSHIP ATTRIBUTES

Communication—The organization now has many constituencies and many observers. Communicating with these groups using the content, form, and channel appropriate for each is both necessary and wise. The leader needs to be verbally articulate, emoting sincerity and displaying concern for the specific constituency and its needs and views and providing situational updates and immediate short-term plans. An extensive vocabulary is an asset, and writing ability, or at least skill in identifying good writing, is also beneficial. Let us provide an example. A number of position holders interact with advertising, public relations, and promotional agencies. Many of these position holders can identify what they do not like when discussing an idea, reviewing copy, or viewing an image. They are not, however, able to articulate to the agencies what they do want. There is a lack of communicational (and perhaps mental) clarity. Consequently, considerable time is spent, and lost, due to the inability of a position holder to clearly express a concept. Good implementer leaders, however, have strong written and verbal communication skills.

Determination—Determination is the relentless pursuit of accomplishment, of getting the job done irrespective of the obstacles one encounters. A leader's sense of determination is infectious to others within the organization and can cascade to all levels. This does not mean a leader needs to affect a grimacing, tight-lipped, glazed-eye visage, which could be counterproductive, but it does mean the leader should have a constant commitment to achieving the objectives without hesitation, faltering, or self-doubt.

Quality-mindedness—In the construction stage there is usually more attention paid to pleasing the market than to internal efficiencies. The organization needs customers. Pleasing and satisfying the market is important, and the quality of the product/service is critical. These factors usually take precedence over cost control in this relatively incipient stage. This is not to say cost control and operational efficiencies are unimportant, but hard choices need to be made at this stage, and quality needs to be a top priority. You can efficiently cost-control yourself out of business if you overadminister, underserve, and disappoint your markets.

Problem-solving—Nothing (that we are aware of) ever goes exactly according to plan. Problems will crop up, new issues will appear, and challenges can and do arise. All of these must be dealt with and dispatched fairly immediately. The operational problem-solving capability of the leader is pivotal in this stage in order to work through the quagmire and guide the still relatively small organization into smooth operations. These minor decisions will translate into policy as they repeat themselves. We distinguish between problem-solving now and decision-making at later stages, as the former deals with micromanagement matters and the latter generally refers to macromanagement matters.

Survival of the fittest is not just an aspect of Darwinian theory; it is a keystone stage in organization formation.

STAGE II PRIMARY VULNERABILITIES

The vulnerabilities of Stage I still apply in Stage II, but less so now that the organization has passed into the construction stage. However, in Stage II new vulnerabilities of a different nature appear; these require different leadership attributes to overcome them.

Undercapitalization—Many organizations fail in the construction stage due to the lack of capital, or money. They start without a deep reservoir of funds necessary to sustain them during the initial period before cash flow turns positive. The entrepreneur may not have the resources, partners will not contribute more cash, banks will lend no more or not at all, and other sources of funds dry up. The organization, deprived of its financial lifeblood, collapses. The leader, who now has to implement the construction of the organization, again must ensure that the capital backbone is sufficiently strong to proceed in the future.

Shoddiness—If quality is a critical attribute in Stage II, then its antithesis, shoddiness, is a grave vulnerability that can lead to demise. Too often products of an inferior nature are rushed to market in the name of financial expediency. The product breaks, burns out, stops working, or is otherwise useless, disparaging the creative and constructive effort to capture a market.

Lack of Standards—Closely related to shoddiness, and its bedrock cause, is the absence of well-developed production and/or service standards. While events may be moving quickly and corporate principals intend to establish standards, intervening factors can cause one to not get to it. This can be a fatal blow for the organization, for overcoming a bad experience by customers is much more difficult than correcting conditions that could lead to a bad experience in the first place. For example, for many years the Chevrolet Corvair was caricatured as the "poster example" of a product that was distributed before all the "bugs" were worked out.

Lack of Training—A lack of training goes hand in hand with a lack of standards. It is not unusual for an organization to believe that it has standards but fail to train its personnel to the level of satisfactory and consistent performance against the standards. Many retail organizations espouse their standards in training manuals, audio-visual aids, employee interactive feedback programs, and behavior modeling, but they do not reinforce those standards when employees are on the job.

Stage III—Development (Growth)

LEADERSHIP ROLE: NAVIGATOR

At this point the organizational framework has been constructed—the figurative brain, skeleton, muscles, and organs are functioning—and the entity is ready to grow. This growth can occur in many forms: steady and proportional growth over a period of time; initial rapid growth with a tapering off period; sporadic spurts at certain intervals; or "late blooming" growth, as in those organizations that seem to be on a plateau but suddenly accelerate.

Nurturing during this development period is critical, because resources must continue to flow to the entity. The organization needs its "vitamins," such as funds, personnel selection, market research, quality control, and customer feedback, and its "shots" to preclude potential maladies such as personnel defections, undercapitalization, early oversatisfaction, and excessive overhead leading to imbalance.

All of the leadership skills required in the creation and construction stages remain paramount, but the development stage requires the following additions.

STAGE III LEADERSHIP ATTRIBUTES

Planning—The leadership skills for strategic direction formation and tactical agility must be evident. Although focus on the new concept is important and cannot be obscured, planning skills enlarge the concept so movement can occur in the chosen direction rather than take place in all directions at once. If you do not have a plan, you may get to where you do not want to be.

The assembly, deployment, and maneuvering of organizational resources are the core of tactical decisions, for the organization cannot afford to "lose a war" due to over-attention to a "battle." Thoughtful, but not necessarily protracted, deliberations and calculated risk-taking are the orders of the day.

Administration—At this point of development, administrative skills are called for in greater measure than they were in earlier times. The organization is extant, but systems must be established to control resources—to use them correctly, economically, and efficiently—and to maximize the effectiveness of the total organization. The organization is becoming acclimated to its marketplace and is "learning" the accepted conduct in the environment in which it is enmeshed. Bringing order out of chaos, or at the very least, avoiding dysfunction, is the navigator leader's administrative challenge.

Relationship Building—As the organization continues to grow, the necessity for forging strong ties with the members of the various constituencies becomes more critical. Internal relationships with operating and staff personnel at both the management and non-management levels are necessary to secure loyalty and belief in the organization and its goals. Relationships with external groups such as venture capitalists, potential franchisees, Wall Street (or LaSalle Street or Montgomery Street), and underwriters are important as well. Credibility, persuasiveness, magnetism, sensitivity, and sensibility are essential qualities to project at this stage; the leader must build bridges, not walls.

Educating—Many leaders do not see themselves as educators, but if one defines that term as "one who causes others to learn," then leaders assume a teaching role whether they want to or not. Other employees model themselves after the leader, absorb and act on the leader's words, and relay these words and actions to peers and subordinates. (We distinguish here between education and training. Education is learning to think; training is learning to do. Those concepts are not mutually exclusive, however.)

In the educator role, the leader transmits the organization's core values, worldview, authority base, structure, role definitions, and policies and procedures. In short, the leader is the clear embodiment and dispatcher of the organization's culture, which should be well understood and widely communicated.

STAGE III PRIMARY VULNERABILITIES

The vulnerabilities that lurk in Stages I and II remain as potential pitfalls in Stage III, but these vulnerabilities are less problematic when the organization has become somewhat established in its marketplace. As is true of development in any form, however, in many cases the vulnerabilities that one experiences at this stage are more severe and have longer-term effects than those that were earlier encountered and overcome. The navigator leader needs to take heed of the following vulnerabilities.

Self-satisfaction—When an organization is created and is well on its way toward fuller development, there is often a false exhilaration on the part of the leader that he or she is solely responsible for the success achieved to date and that the interface of the organization and its markets has been mastered. Thus, there can be a sentiment that what will occur in the future will be as easy as the events of the past. Accordingly, a sense of "we've got the magic touch" or "destiny is on our side" begins to pervade the organization, so the leadership becomes self satisfied and unwittingly transmits this aura of false ebullience to others in the organization.

Overconfidence—Leaders must be alert to the organizational plague known as "corporate conceit." This is the disorder wherein the leaders and the people comprising the organization, by word and behavior, or lack thereof, connote that they exist to be served by their customers rather than to serve them. Corporate conceit is a perversion of the time-honored tradition that the customer is always right. The arrogance of early success subverts the motive of satisfying the constituencies, and the erosion of originally professed values and culture begins.

Personnel Paralysis—Upon the creation of an organization and its ensuing development, it is not unusual for leaders to attend to multiple functions themselves and to be surrounded by a small but loyal group of colleagues who comprise the collective core. Unfortunately, as the organization develops, its needs outgrow the capacity of some original employees to participate in the growth of the firm. These employees either reach a level of competence beyond which they would retard the organization's growth, or for other reasons, such as family commitment or aversion to travel, do not measure up or choose not to keep up with the galloping organization. Often, such employees fail to recognize or otherwise deny these limitations. For example, a bookkeeper is hired initially, but the organizational need becomes one of having a certified public accountant, which, in turn, evolves into a need for a chief financial officer.

The navigator leader must take action at the appropriate time, or the organization will suffer a palsy that restricts its future. The leader knows that the most difficult decisions of all are personnel decisions, but also realizes that the most compassionate thing one can do is to cut someone loose early on when limitations become apparent rather than let a personnel situation linger to the detriment of the entity.

Stage IV—Expansion (Experience)

LEADERSHIP ROLE: ACCELERATOR

The organization is now squarely established and needs to cover additional territory quickly. There are different models for expansion, such as franchising, internal growth, public or private placement, and debt or equity issuance; each model carries with it unique requirements and structures that need leader attention. Expansion can occur concentrically, rippling out from a center core, or diffusely, where random spots of opportunity exist in no prepatterned formation. The pace of the roll-out is important to preempt would-be competitors but not so uncontrolled as to overreach beyond what can be readily grasped. All of the leadership attributes of the earlier stages are required in Stage IV, but in addition, leaders also need the following.

STAGE IV LEADERSHIP ATTRIBUTES

Delegation—Because the organization is moving into new territory, the leader needs to delegate authority (not responsibility) to trusted subordinates in order to effect the objectives stated in the strategic plan. Judgments related to geographical locations, human resource selection, and development, financial arrangements, purchasing, and supply relationships, and use of technology all play a key role in successful expansion. It is at this stage that the leader must have faith in those selected to fulfill the various roles coincident with expansion. Consultants are often engaged at this point to take advantage of their marketplace expertise, contacts, and operational know-how without adding expensive overhead to the organization. Delegation is predicated on trust in individuals, and while disappointments can and do occur, successful leaders have a knack for picking responsible people for appropriate positions and letting them exercise their expertise unfettered by overly close supervision. Micromanagement does not work in rapidly expanding organizations.

Forcefulness—As the organization is now on a rapid acceleration track, the leader needs to be strong minded, strong willed, and strong in restraint as the situation dictates. A regional, national, or world roll-out brings with it new challenges, and the leader's sheer driving force, undaunted by obstacles, is key to perpetuating the momentum. The leader's focus is movement and progress unencumbered by the past.

Pragmatism—While delegation and forcefulness are pivotal components of the leader's character in this stage, they must be supported by a resilient pragmatism. The expansion stage is usually accompanied by supreme optimism on the part of subordinates. Although this is an admirable attitude, it is often also accompanied by ideas that may be whimsical or inappropriate for the particular time. The leader must remain firmly grounded in the organization's best interests and should not leap to fanciful speculation because something sounds good or theoretically possible. Pragmatism should not be confused with pessimism, but it should be allied with realism.

Achiever—Expansion must proceed according to plan, remembering that setbacks inevitably will occur. The leader's achievement record must be evaluated and matched against the plan. The "can do," "will do," and "have done" mantras that underscore the leader's self-concept are transferred to the organization's functioning. Metaphorically, the leader is the accelerator that sets the speed for the organization, recognizing road hazards (competitive forces) and sign limits (governmental regulations). The achiever is not blindly ambitious; he or she is sublimely ambitious.

Stage IV also has elements of organizational tragedy, which, of course, exist in all stages. The primary vulnerabilities that exist in this stage are as pernicious as those in all other stages.

STAGE IV PRIMARY VULNERABILITIES

Profligacy—In the expansion stage the race is on to make as much product or service as possible available for consumption by the constituencies. The focus is often on getting to market first before competitors have a chance to establish their presence. Consequently, resource waste can occur, controls of various forms can be and are overridden, and excessive funds are thrown into advertising, public relations, and promotions. Certainly a balance point must be reached between helter-skelter expansion and constricted expansion, but in most instances organizations err by doing too much rather than too little. The leader needs to exercise strict control so he or she does not waste resources that will be needed according to scheduled time periods.

Overreaching—Most organizations spread their expansion outward from their home-base so headquarters personnel can be on the scene quickly in the event of a problem. There is the danger, however, that geographical expansion to distant markets will result in concept/product/service distortion, inconsistency, waste, and insensitivity to differences in varying marketplaces. The effect is to have a damaged image and reputation and to be regarded as an intruding outsider.

Inflexibility—As the concept creation, construction, and development have occurred, appropriate systems, controls, policies, processes, and procedures have attached to the organization along that journey. This is desirable for certain purposes but can be unnecessarily restrictive in other circumstances. Inflexibility can result in being denied access to certain areas, zoning restrictions for example, or in a reduced level of business activity. Regionalization, as an antidote to nationalization, may be called for to optimize expansion ability, as long as it does not undermine the fundamental tenets of the organization's success to date. Flexibility without deformation is essential.

Defections—At this point in the life of the organization, personnel defections often occur. Although defections can occur at any stage, they become more frequent once more copycat firms are formed to cash in on a proven concept. Key people in the organization are often approached by competitors and the attractiveness of the offer may be tempting to some. Other employees may feel they now have the training and experience to go out on their own with a similar concept. Accordingly, they depart and must be replaced. This is human nature to some extent, but the organization cannot allow mass defections or a continuing sequence of high-level defections or else expansion could slow or stall. Loyalty incentives, such as stock options, need to be in place to deflect defections of these kinds.

Stage V—Cultivation (Maturity)

LEADERSHIP ROLE: HARVESTER

Although an organization should never stop expanding, whether in additional units, new products, new concepts, or product/service line extensions, full maturity of the original concept does occur. The organization reaps the benefits of its earlier progression, and at this point it is at the "top of its game" in its markets. At this stage the leader needs to have the ability to maximize revenue, minimize expenses, increase productivity, and exemplify the positive virtues of one who is in charge of a major economic entity. Although many personal and professional attributes are called for in this stage (building on earlier stages), there are four attributes we identify as primary in Stage V.

STAGE V PRIMARY ATTRIBUTES

Competitiveness—At this point the mature organization has many industry and nonindustry competitors. Industry competitors work in the same type of business. For example, McDonald's competes with Burger King, Wendy's, Jack in the Box, Hardee's, and Carl's Jr. They are all basically hamburger chains, even though they offer other commodities on their menu boards. An extension of their competition comes from other food service industry purveyors of chicken (KFC and Church's Chicken), pizza (Pizza Hut, Domino's, and Papa John's), and Mexican food (Taco Bell and Taco Time). Industry pundits refer to food service competition as vying for "share of stomach."

Nonindustry, or marketplace competitors represent competition from outside one's basic business. For example, on Valentine's Day the floral industry would like you to send flowers to your valentine. The confectioners want you to send candy, and the toy makers want you to send a "huggy bear" or similar furry object. These are different industries, but they compete outside as well as inside their respective industries. Essentially, there are industry competitors and marketplace competitors each vying for the consumer's dollar and loyalty.

The harvester leader can compete in price, perceived value, service, comfort, durability, and/or safety, but he or she must have a competitive niche and must constantly plow the markets for maximum return.

Consistency—A major challenge to leaders at the cultivation stage of an organization's life cycle is keeping the product/service that propelled its success consistent. Quality assurance and inspection standards must be in place and well enforced. Many of the original employees may have retired or left for other reasons, and the replacements may not have the same sense of destiny, growth, excitement, and satisfaction. It is just a job to many of those who now come aboard, and their attention to standards may not be received with the fervor of the original crew. Yet, consistency is necessary to meet the expectations of the marketplace. An inconsistent product or service will drive customers away. It should be noted that consistency is not the same as inflexibility; it is uniformity with room for desired adaptation.

Charisma—As the leader of a major entity, the harvester leader will have a natural charisma simply by virtue of the office held. Major executives seem to radiate an aura of power and style, simply because others sense their level of importance. In addition, however, the leader needs to possess and convey a persona of physical attractiveness and personal magnetism. Physical attraction stems from proper grooming (no ponytails or visible tattoos), quality dress (color-coordinated, conservative outerwear), and a confident body carriage. Personal magnetism is predicated on alert and sparkling eyes, a ready smile, making eye contact, and a positive and complimentary parlance as part of general conversation. A wide vocabulary and strong verbal communication skills add to the individual's "glow."

Character—As a spokesperson, societal opinion leader, powerful position holder, media target, and general exemplar, the harvester leader needs to exhibit a sterling character at all times in front of all constituencies. The leader cannot subject himself or herself to personal or professional suspicion or criticism based on questionable or unseemly behavior. Such a leader must be above reproach, never yielding to temptations. A true leader is both a leader *in* life and a leader *for* life. Counterfeit leaders are usually exposed at some point, and when they are, it tarnishes the organization, sometimes irreparably.

The primary vulnerabilities that are associated with Stage V of the organizational life cycle can exist at any stage, but are likely to make their appearance more intensely and with greater consequences in this stage than at any other point. Recalling that the organization is mature at this stage, the harvester leader should not be susceptible to the following offenses.

STAGE V PRIMARY VULNERABILITIES

Entropy—One law of physics—that a body at rest tends to remain at rest—is true in the organizational world as well. As the entity cultivates its marketplace, it can tend to run on automatic pilot without doing anything new, different, or exciting. The leader needs to avoid organizational complacency, ennui, and lethargy and cannot lose the desire for continuing improvement that should be embedded into the organizational culture. In mathematics any number times zero is still zero; in organizations, doing nothing is still nothing.

Erosion—Erosion is the wearing away or slippage of the core concept and the execution that is required to maintain high standards and continuing customer acceptance. An organizational lethargy can invade the entity as work at the operation becomes perfunctory and a generalized sentiment of "same old, same old" permeates both management and nonmanagement. When this happens, there is a lack of fresh thinking and spirit of renewal. The organization's values are regarded with passivity, if, in fact, they are regarded at all. The organization is on a descending path but does not realize it until profits become affected and customers begin to walk.

Egotism—The harvester leader often succumbs to flattery, media attention, industry recognition, and overproportionate community involvement as nutrients for egotism. The leader may bask in the adulation of the constituencies and fail to recharge subordinates with challenges for increased creativity, productivity, and motivation. A desire for personal attention, myopia with regard to shifting trends, and a lack of attention to signs of internal decay have befallen many a harvester leader.

S tage VI—Renewal (Legacy/Decline)

LEADERSHIP ROLE: EXPLORER

When an organization reaches this stage in its life cycle it faces a crossroads. Superior organizations that have been fortunate to have visionary, mentally tough, and stable leadership have a legacy for future success. The leader in this stage is an explorer who looks for new opportunities both inside and outside the field of current endeavor. The explorer leader has laid the foundation for successor leadership by allowing subordinates to exercise and reach their potential in service to the organization. The organization continues its record of excellence while plowing new ground for regeneration and reinvigoration.

The alternative, the vulnerable organization, continues to decay and ceases to exist, is merged with another organization, or departs from its original business, venturing into other areas. Think of firms such as Howard Johnson restaurants, American Motors, Smith Corona, and NCR, or any of the other well-known corporations that have virtually vanished from the American business landscape. While there are many reasons for the fall of such entities, there is little doubt that with more imaginative leadership and a culture of leadership development, they could still be extant.

The primary attributes of the explorer leader are those which are necessary to keep the organization ascending to new and greater heights. They are as follows.

STAGE VI PRIMARY ATTRIBUTES

Opportunist—The explorer leader, ever alert to the world of commerce, takes advantage of opportunities that he or she creates or observes. Sometimes fortuitous world events, such as the collapse of the Berlin Wall, the demise of the Iron Curtain, or the opening of China, precede opportunities. Opportunity abounds for organizations to serve new and previously underserved populations with products or services that are well established in the Western Hemisphere. The opportunity and the propulsion into new markets portend a growth legacy for the explorer leader; the plowing of new territory or the same territory with new products and services can leave a lasting imprint as part of the explorer's bequest.

Inquisitive—The curious, unsatisfied mind of an explorer leader results in inquiries about new technologies, markets, systems, and products. Being ever alert, active, and inquisitive are the hallmarks of the leader at this stage. Light or extensive travel may be required of the leader to get a firsthand look at the object of interest.

Researcher—The explorer leader has a deep respect for research in all facets of the business. Research that can foretell coming trends, product/service innovation and improvement, and changing marketplaces is fully supported and encouraged by the leader. Consistent with the inquisitive and opportunistic nature of the individual, acquisitions of other organizations are often a priority for this type of leader. The successful explorer leader does not shy away from possible failure but considers failures that may occur as an expected, but manageable, features of organizational renewal.

Ambassador—The explorer leader is the organization's goodwill ambassador. An explorer leader frequently receives accolades for outside roles, such as university trustee, chair of the local United Way Campaign, or honorary or working chair of charitable or political fundraising events. The organization benefits from such activities by absorbing the reflected glory heaped on its leader.

The attributes of leaders in each stage of the organization are neither fixed in time nor discrete for only one given stage; they spill over into different stages. Indeed, it would be ideal if every leader possessed all 27 of the attributes we have identified for the six stages. Similarly, the primary vulnerabilities that occur in one stage can readily appear at any other stage and with sufficient intensity can damage or even sink the organizational ship.

The primary vulnerabilities at the renewal stage are particularly onerous, as they can start the organization on a decline that may be irreversible. If that occurs, the organization is a candidate for merger or extinction. The explorer leader must avoid all of the earlier-mentioned snares in addition to the three that follow.

STAGE VI PRIMARY VULNERABILITIES

Risk Aversion—Pessimists say "it's never a good time to go into business" and back up the statement with negative facts, figures, statistics, economic history, and forecasts. Optimists say "it's always a good time to go into business" and support the statement with an array of positive information. In the renewal stage, the pivotal part of the word (and concept) "renewal" is "new." If the leader is overly cautious and more interested in preservation than in investment opportunities (even though they carry risk), the organization can overprotect itself on its descent. The organization needs to ensure that its explorer leader has the nerve and verve to take chances; the explorer leader cannot be a risk-averter.

Carelessness—The explorer leader still needs to pay attention to the base business. One cannot allow all the honors and adulation that may surface to be a distraction from one's fundamental responsibility—the renewal and continued propulsion of the entity. Inattention can lead to erosion of standards, deteriorating quality, a waning culture, and other organizational maladies that spell "DOOM" (Don't Offend Our Markets).

Vegetation—A sure route to decline is the mental (and physical) laziness of the "sleepy" organization. The "explorer" leader knows that becoming comfortable means becoming vulnerable. Consistent with the renewal stage, the "explorer" leader must keep the organization refreshed and anticipate the dynamics of the future. A vegetating organization is usually a vacillating organization which can evolve into a vulnerable organization and eventually a vanishing organization.

As we conclude Part II, The Life Cycle, we recall the insights from Part I, The Individual, as applied to the schema developed in Part II. We now look to Part III, The Organization, to discuss the leadership elements of entities, and how they present, position, and promote themselves.

Successful Leadership Is:

20%	Vision
20%	Courage
20%	Persona
20%	Timing
20%	Luck

William P. Fisher, Ph.D.

The function of leadership is not to get others to favor you but to get others to follow you!
Christopher C. Muller, Ph.D.

Part III

Leadership:
The Organization

■　　■　　■　　■　　■　　■　　■　　■　　□　　□

Some organizations are transformed by the individuals who lead them.
Some organizations transcend the individuals who purport to lead them.

William P. Fisher, Ph.D.

The only thing more dispiriting than inept followers is inept leaders.

Christopher C. Muller, Ph.D.

Institutions as Organizations

In the English language, the word "institution" has multiple meanings depending on the context in which it is used. In the sociological sense, "institution" is a noun that describes a norm, which is an acculturated and widely accepted state of being or occurrance. Marriage is an example of a sociological institution. The singing of the National Anthem prior to major sporting events and the celebration of the Macy's Thanksgiving Day Parade in New York City are also institutions in this sense.

On another level, people often refer to an edifice or a collection of edifices as an institution. Our universities and colleges are referred to as institutions of higher learning. Facilities where people are detained or committed are referred to as penal institutions and mental health care institutions, and the residents are said to be "institutionalized."

For the purpose of understanding the concept of leadership as it is practiced by organizations, we need to reaffirm what we mean by an "organization" since these entities exert institutional leadership. **An organization is a system of processes and relationships between and among interconnecting individuals, usually within a hierarchy, who function in prescribed positions with specific duties. The coordination and cumulative effort of these duties is directed toward a planned, stated, written mission and objectives.** Essentially, an organization is a system of relationships. It is not a building, a chart, a diagram, simply a name, or a single person.

As we transition from our discussion of the person as a leader and the organization life cycle, we need to consider the organization as a leadership force in its relation to society, its environment, and its competition. Organizations can be leaders as much as people can, and we will investigate the leverage points possessed by different organizations which set these organizations apart from the clutter of the total environment.

Organizational Leadership Leverage Points

Just as a person possesses leadership attributes and vulnerabilities, an organization may be characterized by phrases such as "an industry leader," "a dominant player," a "good company," or other suitable euphemisms. Conversely, organizations that have succumbed or are in the process of succumbing to one or more vulnerabilities are often characterized as "laggards," "moribund," "unimaginative," or "struggling."

This fact should not be surprising, because any organization is reflective of its human leadership. Essentially, good leaders equal good organizations, and bad leaders equal bad organizations. It is thus crucial to have the right leader in place at the right time (remember the life-cycle concept). A beneficial match expedites success, and an ill-advised match hastens decline.

Organizations that succeed over the long term flourish as the result of fortuitous early leadership on the part of their founder(s), who carefully craft and nurture a vision, mission, and culture that become ingrained in the organizations' constituencies. One need only look at the framers of the Declaration of Independence and the Constitution of the United States to see one of the most compelling and vivid examples.

Corporations that have been (or will be) successful over time usually have one or more leverage points. The leverage point is no guarantee of success if other factors, such as poor leadership, work against the organization, but it does give the organization a "leg up" on the competition if the organization is led and managed well.

We have identified 20 institutional leadership leverage points that give the named organizations in each of the following categories a disproportionate advantage over organizations that lack these points. We fully recognize the dynamic nature of the economic and political marketplace and that cataclysmic changes, such as the demise of the Soviet Union and the formation of the European Union, do occur from time to time. By and large however, these leverage points, and the organizations that possess them, have stood the test of time.

Many of the organizations discussed and named in the following pages could fit into two or more categories, because they possess multiple leverage points, fortifying them further. We have intentionally avoided duplication in favor of identifying more and different types of organizations to exemplify the leverage category. As you review the categories, no doubt you will be able to think of other organizations that fit just as well. There is no priority or "weighting" in the order of the categories as listed. Each is discrete and significant in its own right.

LINEAGE

At this point in commercial business history, there are a number of organizations that retain the surname of their founders. Often, these people groomed their family members to be heirs and successors of the organization they founded as well as the beneficiaries of their estates.

Consider Marriott International, for example. J. Willard Marriott, with enormous support from his wife, Alice, founded the organization that bears his name and is now run by his oldest son, J. Willard Marriott, Jr. Starting as a root beer stand, the organization proceeded through the cycles of the food service business, including Hot Shoppes Restaurants and contract feeding, to become one of the premier lodging companies in the world. Marriott stumbled, however, when it attempted to enter other industries, such as amusement parks, cruise lines, and retirement residences. Fortunately, Marriott's leadership was stable enough to weather those economic storms. There is a picture of father and son in the lobby of every Marriott property to show the world that Marriott is a family name. As Bill Marriott, Jr., is fond of saying, "We've got to be good because our name is on the door."

Not to be outdone, Hilton Hotels Corporation is named after its founder, Conrad Hilton, and is now headed by Hilton's oldest son, Barron. Portraits of these men also reside in the lobbies of Hilton properties, suggesting that "flesh and blood" is the backbone of a diverse, international corporation.

The Ford Motor Company bears the name of its founder, Henry Ford. It is now, once again, being run by a member of the Ford family, William Clay Ford, Jr., great-grandson of Henry.

Other organizations that carry the readily recognizable names of their founders include Dell; Hewlett-Packard (HP); L. L. Bean; Marshall Field's; Baskin-Robbins; Coors Brewing Company; Harry & David; H. J. Heinz; Merrill Lynch, and Co., Inc.; J. C. Penney; and H & R Block.

The name, and often the progeny heritage, of these companies provides a marketplace consciousness that the founders, often legendary in their respective industries, began and cultivated organizations and set conditions for their leadership that endure to the present day.

Family members in leadership roles provide a powerful presence that translates into institutional leadership. In other circumstances, however, some venerable founder or cofounder names have passed from the scene through demise or merger. You may or may not recall the names of Montgomery Ward, Fanny Farmer, E. F. Hutton, Kresge, Edsel, Gimbel's, Stromberg-Carlson, and Nash.

SERVICE

A number of organizations exercise their leverage through their reputation for service. They have inculcated in their employees a sense of putting customers first and foremost. This often leads to stories of exceptional service acts that have occurred by employees going out of their way to ensure customer satisfaction.

One of the foremost service culture organizations is the Nordstrom department store chain. Nordstrom's secret of success, in part, lies in selecting people who genuinely enjoy being of service to others and in conducting thorough initial and ongoing training programs for employees. Employees perform random acts of service without hesitation, to the delight and benefit of customers.

The Ritz-Carlton Hotel Company also enjoys a deserved, solid reputation for great service. The company motto, which every one of its employees can recite, is "Ladies and gentlemen serving ladies and gentlemen." Company officials relate to their employees with the utmost dignity and respect and expect them to carry that attitude into their positions, both in their interactions with hotel guests and with one another.

Four Seasons Hotels and Resorts are also known for their service culture, strong focus, and their attention to employee recruitment, selection, orientation, and training.

Sears, Roebuck and Company, usually referred to as "Sears," likewise has a sterling reputation for customer service. Generally, if a customer is dissatisfied in any way with a product purchased at Sears, he or she can return it for a refund with no questions asked. This policy is equally applicable to Sears catalog department sales as to retail store sales.

Other high-service level organizations include Singapore Airlines, for the quality of its service and food; Enterprise Rent-A-Car, which will send a representative to pick you up at your location if you require it; USAA, which provides financial products and services for members of the military and their families; and Wachovia, a consumer banking company.

SAFETY

Some industries operate by an unwritten law that states they will not use safety as a leverage point, because it would adversely affect both the industry and their business. A case in point is the commercial airline industry. Commercial airlines do not promote their safety records as part of their outreach to the public, rightly believing that raising safety as an issue could backfire and reduce air travel for all airlines. Safety statistics for airlines are available, however, from both the federal government and the industry's association, the Air Transport Association (ATA). The statistics indicate that on a per-passenger, per-mile basis, flying is notably safer than driving.

Other industries do emphasize safety features as part of their advertising and promotion to the marketplace. The Volvo Car Corporation emphasizes "world-class safety" in its literature, whereas other automobile manufacturers choose to emphasize style, creature comfort, gas economy, ruggedness, or other features. Statistics and facts are used to document such safety claims.

The Michelin Tire Company emphasizes safety in a more subtle manner, using images of 15–18-month-old infants in its advertisements, suggesting that the safety of the consumer's family is the company's concern.

QUALITY

Quality is a leverage point that is both used and abused by a number of companies. If one defines quality as the essential nature of a product or service that is free from defects and ranks higher than others in its milieu, then leading companies hold quality as a desirable attribute. While all firms strive for quality, a few have attained recognition among consumers as being consistently conscious of quality.

Hallmark Cards is an organization that has a strong record of quality imaging. The firm emphasizes family values and sponsors critically acclaimed television shows that often run without commercial interruption. Its spokespersons (usually in voice-overs) speak articulately and in dulcet tones. The audio and visual image of its products is one of refinement. Hallmark's company slogan, "When you care enough to send the very best," is indicative of its company image and culture.

The primarily ice cream products of Ben & Jerry's Homemade Holdings have a reputation of quality, based on their "taste feel". Ben & Jerry's uses a higher level of butter fat in its base product than do competitors. This difference provides a salutary taste benefit to the consumer.

A more indirect and subtle projection of a quality proposition is expressed by Maytag, the appliance manufacturer. Maytag has enjoyed long-term success with its "lonely repairman" campaign. In both print and broadcast media, a uniformed repairman sits by the telephone waiting for a maintenance call, which never comes. The message, of course, is that Maytag products are so well made that they do not break down.

VALUE

Many organizations seek to gain and retain customers by emphasizing value. We define value as the distinctive component of a product or service which offers exceptional utility, merit or worth beyond that of competitors.

Volkswagen automobiles have long emphasized value. First arriving in the United States in the mid-1900s, their ubiquitous pale blue color, small curvilinear shape, and nicknames, "Beetle" or "Bug", made the cars a cult product on the nation's roadways. Currently, Volkswagen's variety and economy of models, lack of pretense, strong promotional messages, and desire to forge a strong bond among Volkswagen owners suggest that the company is reaching back to its cult origin.

The American Association of Retired Persons (AARP) is an association of older Americans that offers products and services at extraordinarily reasonable prices. One is eligible for membership upon reaching the age of 50, when many people begin thinking of retirement and when medical maladies begin to occur with increased frequency and severity. A one-year AARP membership costs $12.50 (U.S.), and a three-year membership costs $29.50. The association offers various insurance products, pharmaceuticals at a substantial discount, travel discounts, a magazine, advice on financial matters, advice on wills and estates, and a variety of other benefits. It has a tremendous membership, in the tens of millions and growing, because it offers significant value to a constituency that is eager for its services.

Some organizations put the word "value" in their corporate names to incisively convey their value propositions to the marketplace. TrueValue hardware stores and SuperValue grocery stores are two such examples.

CACHET

Cachet, or status, is an aspiration of many organizations. These organizations appeal to customers' egos, making them feel "high class," a "cut above," or "with it," as compared to others.

In the apparel industry, Ralph Lauren has been associated with the polo player, as the image of the horse and rider adorns much of the clothing produced under his label. When Ralph Lauren started out, he had no personal affinity to the sport of polo, but other sports, particularly contact sports such as football, soccer, and baseball, seemed inappropriate. Because he wanted to market more than just swimwear, a diver or swimmer was not wholly appropriate either, and Speedo products already employed a swimming logo. The polo player logo has become a status symbol that has been applied to other products, such as men's aftershave and cologne, luggage, and animal clothing. The success of the polo player led to other brands, most notably RL and another less expensive line of apparel, Chaps. Both males and females are attracted to these brands.

Tommy Hilfiger entered the apparel industry some years after Ralph Lauren and created his own cachet. Hilfiger's primary emblem is a "ribbon" of white on the left and red on the right encased in a blue frame. This emblem has grown in popularity to rival the polo player logo, and both of them outdistance the earliest entrant to the cachet leverage category, Lacoste, with its alligator emblem. Hilfiger also has a "crest," as does Ralph Lauren, but with apparent unabashed humility he puts his name, "Tommy Hilfiger" or just "Tommy," on belts, jeans, T-shirts, and other articles of clothing. Nautica is another brand of casual apparel attempting to capture market share based on its cachet.

Other industries, and the firms that comprise them, also try to use the cachet leverage point advantage. Auto makers Cadillac, Lincoln, Rolls-Royce, Mercedes-Benz, and Jaguar all market their products as the pinnacle car for those who have "made it."

Distillers also use this leverage point. Beefeater gin, Chivas Regal scotch, Bacardi rum, and Baileys digestif are all high-priced, advertised to appeal to the affluent consumer who expects, is used to, and wants to project to others the "finer" things in life.

PRICING

One of the oldest leverage points for organizational leadership is a bargain price. Retail megastores such as Wal-Mart, The Home Depot, Lowe's, Big Lots!, and Best Buy take advantage of this leverage point. Often, derivative organizations of these "major players" also feature low prices. Sam's Club is one derivative of Wal-Mart, named after their founder, Sam Walton. Sam's Club, and other "clubs" like it, such as Price Club and Costco, charge shoppers a fee to enter the premises, and one's membership card is checked at the door to preserve the integrity of the club feature. Because many products are packaged in bulk, the lower packaging costs translate to a lower per-unit cost for the consumer.

Southwest Airlines is a low-price, no-frills airline that continues to succeed at a time when other carriers are losing millions of dollars. The upbeat attitude and humor of the crew overcomes the lack of food service, snacks excepted. Southwest takes reservations but does not make seating assignments until passengers are at the gate and in line. It does not make connecting flights with other airlines or with itself; making relatively short (less than three hours) point-to-point flights only. Southwest pilots only fly Boeing 737s. Herb Kelleher, the airline's co-founder, is regarded as a lovable maverick by business admirers, a tough competitor by other airline industry executives, and a sought-after, witty speaker by associations and other business groups.

Outlet stores are becoming increasingly popular with shoppers as name brand manufacturers place their goods—often out of season or slow-moving items—in these units, where prices are reduced relative to standard stores. Some mall developers specialize in building outlet centers and attract name brand tenants. Prime Outlets and Belz are two such organizations.

SIZE

While an unusual illustration for a book of this nature, the Roman Catholic Church is one of the best examples of an organization that uses size as a leverage point. With more than a billion members the Roman Catholic Church is an institution of enormous size, influence, and wealth. In terms of organizational leadership, the Pope carries great weight with governments, businesses, and other religious leaders around the globe. The papal selection process (leader identification) is conducted by a College of Cardinals, who, presumably, elect the best leader based on criteria determined by the needs of the Church at the current time. The reach of the organization is extensive; this is the cornerstone of its leverage in the world at large.

American Express is another institution with tremendous size and global reach. Its presence in nearly every country in the world helps keep it in consumers' minds as a credit card company. However, American Express is an integrated financial services firm with many lines of business beyond credit and debit cards, including travel agencies, travelers check, business consulting assistance, etc. Its size has a significant impact on each of its lines of business and new endeavors. In some instances, its name can represent vulnerability, however. Citizens of other nations who may be nationalistic in their own right, may not have an affinity for a company with "American" as part of its name. Would you be inclined to use a major credit card that was called "French Express" or "Swiss Express"? American Express's major competitors in the card business—Visa, MasterCard, and Discover—do not have this issue.

Other organizations of significant size in their lines of business include Caterpillar, Bechtel, ExxonMobil, and Boeing. Size, as a point of leverage for an organization, can prove to be enduringly dominant.

CONVENIENCE

In a time-starved world, convenience is a feature that is sought after by most consumers. Recent reports indicate that meals prepared at home are declining in favor of restaurant or take-out meals. The time devoted to cooking at home, when it occurs, averages 30 minutes or less.

Taking advantage of the trend, supermarkets are enlarging their delicatessen and prepared foods departments, and restaurant organizations such as Boston Market (owned by McDonald's) advertise entire "home meal replacement (HMR)" dinners as part of their strategies.

Domino's Pizza scored a leadership breakthrough when it began home delivery with a "30-minute guarantee." After some automobile liability claims filed because drivers were racing to meet or beat the guarantee, the firm had to relinquish its guarantee. Nonetheless, home pizza delivery was quickly adopted by other major pizza chains and independent operations.

The convenience store 7-Eleven derived its name from its hours of operation, 7:00 A.M. to 11:00 P.M. The company's strategy was to remain open after other grocery stores closed. In fact, many 7-Eleven units are open beyond those hours. Other major grocery store organizations, such as Albertson's, remain open 24 hours a day, countering 7-Eleven's convenience.

Hertz, a rental car company, instituted a "direct to your (rental) automobile" program a number of years ago to save customers from waiting in line at the registration counter. Other rental car companies quickly followed suit.

The American Automobile Association (AAA) offers its members numerous convenience services, such as insurance, travel reservations, TripTiks, and traveler's checks. Perhaps the organization's most valued and appreciated service, however, is the members' ability to call a AAA station operator who will arrive to tow and repair a disabled vehicle. The convenience of not being stranded repeatedly ranks high in AAA's surveys of member satisfaction.

Starbucks has implemented its own debit card system, so that frequent customers can speed up their coffee purchasing experience. Mobil gas stations introduced Speedpass so gasoline purchases can be automatically recorded and billed to the customer.

Other organizations and products have also tapped the convenience leverage point by bringing products to customers through their distribution system. Mary Kay beauty products are sold in neighborhoods by Mary Kay representatives who invite potential customers into their homes or other suitable locations for "parties." Tupperware also has representatives who hold "Tupperware parties."

Convenience will continue to be a growing leverage point for institutions which have the vision and creativity to take advantage of it. Consumers are demanding it and in highly competitive markets, the customer rules.

Organizations know they need to be more service oriented, and convenience is a primary form of service.

DIVERSITY

Diversity is becoming more of a focal leverage point for organizations than it ever has been before. Diversity refers to the engagement of relationships with multicultural, multiracial, multiethnic and other minority populations encompassing employees, customers, suppliers, and other constituencies. It is good business in an increasingly diverse world. It is not judicial affirmative action.

An institution that is a forerunner for diversity precepts is the U.S. military. Since the edict that mandated desegregation of military units approximately a half-century ago, the Army, Navy, Air Force, Marines, and Coast Guard have pursued diversity as an operational goal. There are no more racially and ethnically segregated military units, and the Women's Army Corps (WACS), Women Accepted for Volunteer Emergency Service (WAVES), and Women's Auxiliary Ferrying Squadron (WAFS) have been consigned to history. Military leadership, by nature and necessity, is tightly structured, authoritarian, and stratified. Diversity in the ranks was not accomplished without difficulties, but it is accepted as commonplace in the service branches today. Diversity within the military has influenced civilian society, and while problems occur on occasion, diversity remains a part of contemporary American life thanks in large part to military leadership.

A number of institutions could be singled out as positive examples of commitment to organizational diversity. Hyatt Hotels Corporation has an outstanding program in which employees are specifically assigned to diversity management issues. These employees conduct extensive training and serve as models for other employees at all levels. Hyatt provides scholarships for minority students and support a number of diversity-oriented community programs around the country. Loews Hotels is another organization that is outstanding in its commitment to diversity.

The nation's public and most of the nation's private universities are intently committed to diversity, particularly when attempting to attract qualified faculty. Governmental agencies embrace diversity, describing themselves as color blind and gender neutral in their human resources policies and procedures. Minority populations have been told they can vote with their dollars and their feet, meaning they can choose not to support organizations lagging in diversity management.

PRODUCT EXTENSION

Product extension expands the same fundamental product or service into several different niches or tiers, whereas brand expansion, discussed in the next section, conveys the name of a recognized entity to another type of product or service.

Nike is a master product extender, as are other footwear organizations. Nike has leveraged its recreational footwear position into a long list of niches. There are rubber-soled shoes, or sneakers, made and marketed specifically for basketball players, soccer players, runners, walkers, volleyball players, hikers, tennis players, and others. Perish the thought that you should purchase and wear the wrong footwear for the wrong sport. A masterful marketer, Nike has created separate footwear markets for separate sports, thereby causing multiple buying opportunities for those who engage in several sporting activities. It should be noted that Nike is also an example of brand expansion because its name and "swoosh" logo appear on apparel, footballs, basketballs, tennis warm-ups, and many other products. Appropriately, in Greek mythology, Nike is the goddess of victory.

H. J. Heinz Company is another familiar example of product extension. Up until a few years ago, the company's ketchup was red and packaged in what became generically known as a "ketchup bottle." Taking advantage of the youth market, the company is now producing ketchup that is burgundy, blue, or green in color because young people like color variety. In addition, ketchup is now packaged in plastic containers so that it can be squeezed out.

Holiday Inn is another product (service) extender. Most of the businesses in the company's portfolio carry the words "Holiday Inn" in the name:

- Holiday Inn
- Holiday Inn Select
- Holiday Inn Sun Spree Resorts
- Holiday Inn Express
- Holiday Inn Garden Court
- Holiday Inn Family Suites

Although the properties are marketed differently to different constituencies, they all represent the same basic product (service): a hotel room.

The retail apparel clothing chain, Gap, also markets to different niches. In addition to "regular" Gap stores, there are GapKids stores, for children age 4 to teens, and babyGap stores, for infants and toddlers.

BRAND EXPANSION

Brand expansion is taking marketplace recognition of an established name and attaching it to different products or services which sometimes are markedly different. Brand expansion is a major leadership leverage point.

General Electric Company (GE) is a prime example. Under the general heading of "household appliances," the GE brand can be found on refrigerators, washers, dryers, microwave ovens, air conditioners, compactors, disposals, and other products. Although each appliance has a different function, the

GE name appears on all of them. In addition, GE is the manufacturer of multiple types of lighting systems, motors, adhesives, and sealers. GE's most profitable unit is GE Credit, a financing arm of the multifaceted organization. As a side note, General Electric also owns some organizations wherein its name is not evident. One of its largest holdings is the NBC television network and its subsidiaries. GE also co-owns Polo.com with Polo's Ralph Lauren.

Disney is another example of brand expansion. Due to the positive reception of Walt Disney's cartoon characters, such as Mickey Mouse and Donald Duck, Disney entered into the amusement/theme park industry, first with Disneyland in California, and then with Walt Disney World in Florida. Disney's theme park business is now an international enterprise, with parks in France and Japan, and one in Hong Kong on the horizon. Disney also owns and operates a cruise line; a vacation club; a radio station; retail apparel and toy stores; and game, video and arts and crafts divisions. Businesses owned by Disney but that do not display the Disney name include ABC (American Broadcasting System) and its subsidiaries, including ESPN. Disney also owns Miramax and Touchstone Pictures motion picture productions.

The Gillette Company is still another vivid example of a brand expander. Starting as a razor blade manufacturer, Gillette now manufactures both permanent and disposable safety razors, shaving cream, toothbrushes, deodorants, and hair spray. Products the company owns in which the Gillette name is not readily apparent are Braun electric razors and Duracell alkaline batteries.

MULTIPLE BRANDING

An interesting leadership leverage strategy is to promote individual product/service brands rather than the institutional name. Howard Johnson is a company that used this strategy. The company, named after its founder, started life as an ice cream restaurant chain. It had a bright, orange-colored roof and was known for its many flavors of ice cream, and later, its mediocre food. It expanded rapidly in the 1950s after World War II, and units could be found in many major cities and along the interstate highway gas and rest stops. The company ventured into the lodging industry with Howard Johnson Motor Lodges. Over time, the restaurant organization began to deteriorate, and a number of restaurant units began losing money. Management made the conscious decision to convert the losing units to another concept called Ground Round. In contrast to Howard Johnson Restaurants' sparkling bright luncheonette/family restaurant image, Ground Round's interior was darker. Diners were greeted with straw baskets of popcorn and unshelled peanuts. (The peanut shells would be thrown on the floor). The menu consisted of hamburgers, hot dogs, and French fries for the most part and the restaurant served beer. It appealed to a younger client with its continuous showing of cartoon loops. It was 180 degrees away from the original Howard Johnson concept, so the company made the deliberate decision NOT to use the Howard Johnson name in connection with the Ground Round to avoid negative spillover from one concept to the other. (Howard Johnson remains a lodging brand, the name of which is owned by Cendant Corporation.)

This example does not suggest that institutions that employ an individual brand strategy do so out of protective anxiety. It does suggest that there are definite benefits in having one's own identity rather than being leveraged under the banner of a corporate Valkyrie.

A well-known example of the multiple brand strategy is General Motors Corporation. While the familiar steel block insignia "GM" does appear on sales material of the company's automobile brands, it is greatly subdued relative to the primary name of the vehicle. The company manufactures Chevrolet, Pontiac, Buick, Cadillac, Hummer, and Saturn (the Oldsmobile is being phased out), but only the GMC division carries the General Motors Corporation connotation, and that group manufactures SUVs. The original General Motors concept was to keep an initial buyer in the "family" by selling a lower priced Chevrolet, and moving that buyer progressively upward to a Pontiac, Oldsmobile, Buick, and Cadillac as he or she aged and got wealthier and the price points of the vehicles moved upward.

Darden Restaurants, Inc., the largest casual dining chain in the world, also employs a multiple branding strategy. There is no "Darden" restaurant brand per se. Rather, their five concepts—Red Lobster, Olive Garden, Bahama Breeze, Smoky Bones, and Seasons 52—are established as their own chains, each pitching to a different market. Few members of the public realize these brands are related through common ownership.

Multiple branding organizational leadership works with the right people with the right qualities in place to run the brands.

ICONS AND SLOGANS

Organizational leadership can be developed with the employment of icons that become part of the national scene and often the cultural folklore. Icons are readily visible and recognizable images that most people can identify through shape and color even when the name of the organization is absent.

McDonald's Corporation is fortunate to have two icons associated with it. The "golden arches" are fixtures in most North American cities and increasingly so in cities around the world. The arches, of course, are an "M" which stands for McDonald's. McDonald's is also represented by a cheerful, colorfully dressed clown named Ronald McDonald who delights children with his antics, puzzles, and toys. (The Ronald McDonald House will be discussed in Part IV.) On the left side of the following table is a list of institutions which employ "iconology." On the right side is a list of icons. Stop for a moment and see if you can recall the icon that depicts the company without looking at the right side list. We will start with an easy one.

Institution or Brand		Icon
1.	Green Giant	Jolly Green Giant
2.	Pillsbury	Dough Boy
3.	Mobil Oil (Now ExxonMobil)	Pegasus (flying horse)
4.	Goodyear	Blimp
5.	Energizer batteries	Energizer Bunny
6.	Pizza Hut	Red Top Hat
7.	Michelin	Tire Man
8.	U. S. Forest Service	Smokey the Bear
9.	Nike	Swoosh
10.	Kellogg's Frosted Flakes	Tony the Tiger
11.	Metro-Goldwyn-Mayer	Roaring Lion
12.	Prudential Financial	Rock of Gibraltar
13.	Travelers Insurance	Red Umbrella
14.	Allstate Insurance	Two "good" hands
15.	Planter's Peanuts	Mr. Peanut

Slogans can also play a leadership leveraging role, because they are usually closely associated with the icon or company insignia. Slogans can become so ingrained in human consciousness that many people can complete the phrase once the first few words are mentioned, or they can exercise total recall of the full statement. Permit us to "test" you with lists once again. On the left side of the following table is the slogan of the organization. On the right side, the organization is identified. Try to read the left list first without looking at the right-side counterpart.

Slogan		Institution or Brand
1.	"A few good men"	U. S. Marine Corps
2.	"We bring good things to life."	General Electric Company
3.	"It's Finger Lickin' Good"	KFC
4.	"You are in good hands with. . ."	Allstate
5.	"Nobody doesn't like. . ."	Sara Lee
6.	"Breakfast of Champions"	Wheaties
7.	"All the News That's Fit to Print"	*The New York Times*
8.	"It's What's for Dinner"	Beef Council
9.	"Cover the Earth"	The Sherwin-Williams Company
10.	"A Title on the door means a . . . on the floor"	Bigelow (carpets)
11.	"Drivers Wanted"	Volkswagen

12.	"That's what —— is, mmm good"	Campbell's Soup
13.	"Like a good neighbor. . ."	State Farm Insurance
14.	"It's everywhere you want to be."	Visa
15.	"The King of Beers"	Budweiser (Anheuser-Busch)

An icon or memorable slogan provides a decided leadership role for an organization in its industry. These images and phrases have become so imprinted on the national psyche that they have become household names, offering considerable economic benefit to the organization.

GENERICS

Some organizations are fortunate to have their name, or the name of one or more of their brand products, become part of the national vocabulary as a generic term. Gelatin is a food product often used for fillings, desserts, and salads. Kraft Foods now owns the brand "Jell-O," which was previously owned by General Foods. Most people believe that "Jell-O" is a commodity name rather than a brand of gelatin, because Jell-O has been so ubiquitous and so successful in emblazoning its brand name in the minds of consumers.

Kleenex is another example. Kleenex, a facial tissue, is a brand owned by the Kimberly-Clark Corporation. The word "Kleenex" is synonymous with facial tissue in the minds of many. It is not unusual to hear someone ask, "May I have a Kleenex?" That person is really asking for a brand, when, in fact, any facial tissue would satisfy the request.

Xerox Corporation was a pioneer in the photocopying industry. In the 1960s the Xerox brand became so prevalent that the term "Xerox" came to mean "photocopy" to many people. "Please make a Xerox of this" was a common refrain heard in offices around the world, even though many other manufacturers of photocopy equipment were operating in the marketplace.

The story of Federal Express (FedEx) is well known in most business quarters. When the company's founder, Fred Smith, was a student at Yale University, he wrote a paper outlining his concept for package delivery by flying all parcels into a central location (Memphis, Tennessee) and redeploying them to their intended destinations. Undeterred by the middling grade he received from his professor, Smith went on to form and grow the company that became Federal Express. Overnight delivery of goods and documents has become commonplace, and it is not uncommon to hear someone say "Here, FedEx this," when they simply mean to send the package overnight.

Another phrase you may hear that has attained generic word status is "I'll have a Coke, please," when the customer is asking for any cola. Restaurants that serve Pepsi-Cola usually instruct their servers to reply "Is Pepsi O.K.?"

"I need some Scotch tape" is another such statement that uses the brand "Scotch" (owned by 3M Corporation) as a synonym for adhesive tape.

You have probably heard the expression "It's as clean as Spic and Span" indicating a supreme degree of cleanliness. Spic and Span is a cleaning agent made by a company of the same name.

The dominance of the product and brand name has become so widespread and achieved such a high level of acceptance by the public that the companies and brands have a superior leadership leverage position.

SERENDIPITY

"Serendipity" is a word that indicates an accidental discovery which turns out to be beneficial. Some people call it tangible luck.

The perfume industry is highly competitive. Many celebrities—Elizabeth Taylor being a prime example—lend their names to fragrances in anticipation of capitalizing on an alluring product.

Considerable research is undertaken by perfume manufacturers to identify desirable perfume scents and to avoid medical liabilities such as rashes and asthma attacks. Several decades ago, Shulton, Inc., was experimenting with fragrances to determine the right formula for a perfume. Nothing seemed to be appealing to the feminine olfactory sense. A male happened to stumble across one concoction, lifted it to his nose, liked the odor, and splashed some on his face. Thus, Old Spice aftershave lotion was born, ushering in a whole new industry of men's toiletries, such as aftershave lotions, colognes, and perfumed soaps.

Another well-known "accidental" discovery occurred within the 3M Corporation (originally known as Minnesota Mining and Manufacturing). The 3M Corporation is a major organization with multiple lines of business, one of the foremost of which is adhesives with which 3M has been markedly successful in attracting significant market share. The 3M research department is always looking for stronger adhesives and new uses for them. At one time experiments were underway to formulate an adhesive that would form an exceptionally strong bond between two objects. At one stage of these experiments, the researchers noticed that their formula did not forge a strong bond, but it stuck slightly and could be peeled off without leaving glue residue. The resulting product was Post-it Notes, which are in the desk drawers and on the documents of hundreds of thousands of office workers around the world.

Many other products and services have been discovered as the result of accidental events that proved beneficial. Plastic products, food products (sauces and salad dressings), and dog walking services are a few among many.

After he discovered and perfected the electric lightbulb, Thomas Edison was asked if the 2,000 failures he experienced in all those attempts did not become discouraging. He calmly replied that he did not experience failure; the discovery was simply a 2,000-step process.

DOMINATION

A number of institutions retain their leadership status because of their massive market share in their industries or subindustries. TIAA-CREF, formally known as Teacher's Insurance Annuity Association-College Retirement Equities Fund, is a financial services organization offering insurance products and mutual funds to the public. As one can tell from its full name, TIAA-CREF's primary market is teachers, professors, researchers, and educational administrators. While the organization is open to the public, it enjoys the vast majority of its business from people connected to education. TIAA-CREF is the dominant player for retirement planning and investment services in the educational community.

Hershey Foods Corporation has a broad line of food products but is most noted for its retail candy products and chocolate syrup. What is often overlooked is Hershey's massive penetration and market share in the institutional market for chocolate syrup. If you order a chocolate milk shake or a chocolate sundae at a restaurant, soda fountain, or ice cream stand, it is likely to be made with Hershey's chocolate syrup. The fact that Hershey, Pennsylvania, a real company town, is named after Milton Hershey, and, by extension, the company he founded, also helps the organization retain its leadership status. Even the streetlights on the main street in Hershey, Pennsylvania, are shaped in the form of chocolate candy kisses.

When you were young, you probably played with paper and crayons, drawing pictures or trying to stay within the lines of preprinted scenes in coloring books. No doubt the brand of crayons you used was Crayola, a venerable product that has been the delight of children for decades.

Some organizations are so large in the scope of their offerings that they become known as "category killers." Toys "R" Us carries all lines of toys produced by all the major toy manufacturers. PetSmart stores carry almost every conceivable item a pet owner could want for domesticated pets.

Other organizations that enjoy such market domination that their leadership leverage is unquestioned include S. C. Johnson and Procter & Gamble (P & G). P & G has many brand leaders, including Tide detergent, in its product portfolio.

LOYALTY

A significant number of organizations enjoy almost obsessive customer loyalty. When American Airlines inaugurated its Frequent Flyer Loyalty Points Program in the early 1980s, it unleashed a stampede by other airlines and other industries to reward customers for their loyalty. Every major airline now has a loyalty rewards program, as do lodging establishments, restaurants, rental car companies, and credit card companies. In such programs, customers are rewarded with free travel, room upgrades, vehicle upgrades, merchandise, and even, in the instance of the Discover Card, cash.

Another approach, used primarily by supermarkets, is to provide a plastic machine-readable bar code chip card that the holder presents to the cashier to receive discounts or savings on the products purchased. Albertson's and Kroger are two of several supermarket chains that have developed such a program.

Individual brands also have developed a loyal following among their customers. Starbucks has an enormous following, who gladly spend four dollars or more for a large cup of coffee. Oshkosh B'gosh is a line of durable children's apparel that has a loyal customer base. Luxury jewelers Tiffany & Co. and Cartier each have their camps of followers, as does publisher Reader's Digest.

Customer data mining is a term that appeared in the marketing lexicon some years ago, as companies began attempting to learn all they could about their customers in order to meet their needs. These efforts, of course, translate into customer loyalty as a powerful leverage point.

Constituent loyalty is often recognized in mergers and acquisitions in the financial sense by the "goodwill" account that represents the value over and above other financial measurements that an acquirer is willing to pay to an acquiree.

ORIGINALITY

Being the first at something is definitely a leverage point for a business. The Hyatt Regency Atlanta, which opened in the 1960s, was regarded as an architectural breakthrough for hotels. The lobby is a large atrium in which guests can walk with a floor-to-ceiling view and a feeling of openness, airiness, and beauty. The glass-encased elevators provide passengers with an interior view of the lobby area as they ascend to the upper floors. Other Hyatt Hotels, as well as other brands, have properties that followed suit, but Hyatt has become identified with architectural flair and originality.

When Charles Schwab graduated from Stanford with an MBA, he knew he wanted to enter the stock brokerage business. At the time there were several investment houses including Merrill Lynch et al., E. F. Hutton, and Carl M. Loeb Rhodes, all of which did business in much the same way. The brokerage business was a very personal business. One found a trustworthy broker and bought and sold stocks or bonds through that person, with the broker collecting fees on both buying and selling transactions. The brokerage firms also had (and still do) research departments where analysts poured over reports so brokers could give expert advice to their clients.

Schwab realized that a number of customers did their own research (such as it was) or simply knew the stock they wanted to buy or sell without going into a lot of the background. Accordingly, he opened his discount bro kerage firm, Charles Schwab and Co., charging customers lower than standard broker fees because he did not invest in the research overhead of the conventional brokers of the time. Today, of course, there are numerous discount brokerage houses, but Charles Schwab and Co. continues to be the prominent name in the discount field. Schwab was the original discounter in the stock brokerage business.

Mattel Inc., a toy manufacturer, has enjoyed decades of success with its Barbie doll, as it was the first toy maker to perceive that little girls wanted something more than traditional baby dolls. Barbie sparked a whole new industry of apparel and artifacts for dolls, as well as Ken, formerly Barbie's male counterpart. Mattel has recently produced Emme, a full-figured doll whose measurements are more robust than those of the svelte Barbie. Using self-competition to capture a wider swath of the market is not a new strategy. Depending on which one you choose—of course you are encouraged to purchase both—you will still be purchasing from the same manufacturer. Mattel has had its difficulties in the financial markets, but Barbie remains an American icon.

CASH

No discussion of institutional leadership leverage can overlook the fact that the strength of a balance sheet lies in the abundance of cash available, small debt (low financial leverage), or sizeable retained earnings for an organization.

Altria Corporation, formerly named Philip Morris Companies, is the leading tobacco company in the nation, if not the world. Tobacco often has been referred to as a "cash cow." While smoking continues to be an issue in the United States, it is less so in other parts of the world. As an international organization, Philip Morris does very well. Few people realize that it owns Kraft Foods and Kraft International, and for many years owned the Miller Brewing Company.

Kraft Foods produces more than 90 of the nation's leading brand food products, including coffee, soft drinks, salad dressings, cheese, and breakfast cereals. Kraft has grown over the years through both internal development and acquisition, much of it accomplished with the cash backing of its parent company.

Other tobacco companies have bought their way into other industries on the basis of tobacco cash flow. RJR Industries (R.J. Reynolds) is another prominent example.

Microsoft is another "cash-rich" organization that fuels research and development and acquisitions.

Berkshire Hathaway, Inc., chaired by legendary financier, Warren E. Buffet, is a conglomerate that yields considerable cash. It owns GEICO, the largest automotive and casualty insurance company and General RE, a major reinsurer. Insurance company premiums generate considerable cash, which must be managed in a productive and profitable manner. This need is one reason insurance companies of all types—casualty, life, stock, or mutual firms—own real estate; they want to invest those funds in secure holdings.

Berkshire Hathaway owns companies in the carpet and footwear industries as well as jewelry stores, Dairy Queen, and home furnishings and leasing firms. It is a diversified organization with a very solid balance sheet, making it one of the most highly regarded organizations in American business.

We conclude Part III with Berkshire Hathaway and Mr. Buffet, to emphasize the synergistic influence of institutions being led by men and women at various stages in the institution's organizational life cycle.

As is the case with perceptions of individual leaders, 20 of which we discussed in Part I, we conclude with 20 leadership leverage points for organizations. While there are other categories we could mention as well, we believe we have made our point.

Organizational Leadership Leverage Points Summary

Institutions that lead in their fields have one or more of the following leadership leverage points on which their leadership is based.

1. Lineage
2. Service
3. Safety
4. Quality
5. Value
6. Cachet
7. Pricing
8. Size
9. Convenience
10. Diversity
11. Product Extension
12. Brand Expansion
13. Multiple Branding
14. Icons and Slogans
15. Generics
16. Serendipity
17. Domination

18. Loyalty
19. Originality
20. Cash

Good leaders lead leading organizations! Leading organizations develop good leaders!
William P. Fisher, Ph.D.

Organizations abhor a leadership vacuum.
Christopher C. Muller, Ph.D.

Part IV
Leadership:
The Community

■   ■   ■   ■   ■   ■   ■   ■   □   □

Leadership is not an honorary position!

Christopher C. Muller, Ph.D.

Leaders change lives for the better!

William P. Fisher, Ph.D.

Organizational Leadership in the Community

The first stanza of the national anthem of the United States, "The Star-Spangled Banner," concludes with the words "O'er the land of the free and the home of the brave." If we were to update this revered song, we could add the words "and the nation of the generous."

Americans are the most generous people in the world both individually and institutionally. When natural disasters occur, such as floods or hurricanes, or man-made catastrophes like September 11 transpire, there is an outpouring of financial support.

The attitude that one needs to "give back" to society is also embedded in the American business culture. Each year, American corporations provide billions of dollars in goods and services to people in need, to not-for-profit institutions, such as universities and charities, and to community rehabilitation and/or new construction projects.

Organizations give back to their communities in many ways. A number of corporations have established foundations to oversee much of their largesse, but they also provide support to meaningful programs through their operating entities. The following is just a small sampling of the many ways in which organizations contribute to their communities:

- Donate cash and in-kind gifts to schools, the arts, museums, hospitals, charities, and other activities of "good works."
- Provide an organizational employee to a charity for fundraising purposes, such as "loaning an executive" to the business division of United Way campaigns that are held each fall.
- Provide paid time off for employees to work for other bodies, such as school boards and city or county councils.
- Encourage employee-generated fundraisers, such as Girl Scout Cookie campaigns.
- Provide educational scholarships to qualified children of an organization's employees.
- Provide matching gifts on behalf of employees who make donations to their school, college, or university.
- Provide valuable noncash support to a worthy organization, usually an educational institution.
- Provide the products they manufacture or distribute as an in-kind service.
- "Break rate" by charging a lower rate of interest to a group for a worthy cause.
- Contribute services, such as architectural plans or financial advice, to worthy organizations at no cost.
- Provide safety products to the needy. For example, the Ford Motor Company sponsors a program called "Boost America," wherein free car safety seats are supplied to children of low-income families.
- Sponsor nationwide programs, such as literacy programs.
- Recognize excellence by providing scholarships for school activities, such as the All-American Band, the Future Farmer and the Future Teacher of the Year, the national high school debate, and cheerleading championships.

While major corporations usually contribute at the national level, many also authorize their regional offices or units to participate at the local level.

Policies exist to coordinate and control the total process in most instances. Accordingly, companies both large and small will donate to the various United Way Campaigns, sponsor children's or adult amateur athletic teams, adopt local schools, and provide in-kind products or services, such as free hotel stays, restaurant dinners, free cruises, free automobiles, gift certificates, car wash or pet grooming services for auctions, raffles, and similar types of charitable events. The amount and types of contributions are highly creative.

Companies will often sponsor events, speakers, programs, or research projects for industry associations, which are comprised of members who are clients of the company. Credit card firms, soft drink companies, and beer and wine organizations are notably generous in this regard. In times of emergency, restaurant organizations often supply free food to victims and relief workers.

The type of organization, the amount of funds, and the actual recipient(s) of institutional philanthropy often have a personal significance to one or more of the leaders of the organization. A person who was orphaned as a child will often support adoption programs. A person with a disability, or who has a family member with a disability, will provide support to a group that works toward curing the cause of the disability. A senior business executive who has a penchant for, or perhaps a family member who participates in the arts will authorize organizational leadership support for that particular art.

If a founder of an organization or a leader of an organization in the early stages of the life cycle has an inclination toward one or a few philanthropic outlets, the organization will honor the wishes of that person. Over time, however, when the founder/leader leaves the organizational scene, the company often widens its range of benevolence as the firm continues its growth and success. The company is true to the roots of its founder/leader, of course, but changes in societal needs, coupled with organizational expansion in both geography and areas of interest, dictate a broadening of philanthropic considerations.

In this section of *Four-Dimensional Leadership*, The Community, we have selected 25 organizations to profile briefly in terms of their community involvement and outreach.

The organizations we selected are household names, or own brands that are household names, but they are not necessarily the largest in their industries, nor is their level of giving necessarily the largest relative to that of their competitors. They represent the diversity of the many areas organizations support.

We also attempted to diversify geographically and minimized any overlap with organizations mentioned in Part III. Of necessity, there is some overlap— McDonald's, Hilton, Marriott, and Ford, for example—but our purpose is to show additional organizations in a leadership light. In most instances, the companies we profile extend their community involvement well beyond that which we have mentioned, as do many other companies which space disallows us to include. In order to glean the full scope of what corporations do to give back we recommend that you click on the Web sites of those you wish to view. We believe the information you find there in this regard will well exceed your current general knowledge about these organizations.

A lbertson's

"Albertson's believes in being a good neighbor by contributing to the quality of life in the diverse communities we serve."

(excerpt from Albertson's public relations statement)

Founded in Boise, Idaho, in 1939, Albertson's has become one of the largest retail food and drug chains in the United States. The company operates 2,300 stores in 31 states and employs 200,000 people. The firm owns and operates 19 distribution centers in 11 states. Its slogan, "Albertson's—It's Your Store," reflects the philosophy of its founder, Joe Albertson, who died in 1993 at the age of 86.

Albertson's charitable support is centered in three areas:

HUNGER RELIEF

- Each year, millions of pounds of food and household goods are provided by Albertson's 19 distribution centers to Second Harvest food banks, churches, and local hunger relief organizations.

- Albertson's partnered with the Pillsbury Company and Second Harvest during National Food Bank Week and donated 18 truckloads of food in six markets across America.

- Albertson's provides day-old bakery products to soup kitchens and local food banks.

- The company's Jewel-Osco division donated 25,000 cans of food to *CAN-STRUCTION*, a project sponsored by the Museum of Science and Industry in Chicago. Teams of architects and designers were assembled to build structures using the cans. The canned food was then donated to the Greater Chicago Food Depository.

- Supplies tens of thousands of pounds of canned goods to the Tarrant Area Food Bank, Fort Worth, Texas, in connection with the Adios Hunger project.

YOUTH AND EDUCATION

- Community Partners Card, a partnership between Albertson's food stores and nonprofit youth-oriented organizations, donates a percentage of the grocery store purchases made by supporters of the organization back to the organization.

- The Jewel-Osco division won the Above and Beyond Award granted by Junior Achievement for having store general managers volunteer their time to teach a five-week business course class to students from kindergarten through twelfth grade. More than 300 volunteers taught in 270 classrooms in the Chicago area.

- Albertson's stores in the Houston, Texas, area donated 30,000 pounds of school supplies to local learning programs in the 15 Tons of School Tools program.

- Albertson's stores provide unsubsidized summer jobs for thousands of high-school students each year.

HEALTH AND NUTRITION

- The company is a sponsor for the Lifetime Television for Women's fight against breast cancer, which conveys the "Someone You Know" message.

- Albertson's stores, including Acme, Jewel, Seessel's, and Max Food grocery stores, issue free early breast cancer detection cards.

- The company's Osco and Sav-on drugstore divisions provide free brochures to women on the subject of breast cancer.

- Partnering with other organizations, Albertson's has donated tens of thousands of dollars to the Susan B. Komen Foundation to support finding a cure for breast cancer.

Albertson's also makes its presence felt when tragedies occur. When Littleton, Colorado, was shaken by the Columbine High School shootings, employees immediately prepared and served food and beverages to rescue crews and law enforcement personnel. Albertson's also helped establish and made a significant contribution to the United Way's Healing Fund to help the community overcome the tragedy. In addition, Acme, one of Albertson's divisions, helped raise significant funds for relief efforts made necessary by Hurricane Floyd.

 nheuser-Busch Companies

"The company and its charitable foundations support education programs, provide disaster relief, help preserve the environment, encourage responsible consumption of their products . . . and much more."

> *(from "Making Friends—Making a Difference," a publication of Anheuser-Busch)*

The 152-year-old, St. Louis, Missouri-based Anheuser-Busch company operates in three arenas: brewing, packaging, and entertainment. Perhaps best known for its Budweiser and Michelob brands, the firm commands nearly 50 percent market share of its brewed products. The packaging group includes Metal Container Corporation (cans), Eagle Packaging (crown and closure liner materials), and Longhorn Glass Corporation (bottles), among others. The entertainment group includes various Sea World locations, Busch Gardens, and other parks and visitor attractions.

The company has an extensive community outreach program that has been in existence for decades. Here is a sample of 25 of the more than 200 educational institutions, charities, relief programs, arts, cultural societies, and other philanthropic programs that the company regularly supports:

- American Red Cross
- United Way
- Washington University
- Community Foundation for the National Capital Region
- Urban League
- Saint Louis University
- Cornell University
- 100 Black Men of America
- Boy Scouts of America
- Girls, Inc.
- Jewish Federation
- Cardinal Glennon Children's Hospital
- Paralyzed Veterans of America
- YMCA
- Smithsonian National Air and Space Museum
- National Fish and Wildlife Federation
- Ducks Unlimited
- Mexican American Legal Defense and Education Fund
- Hispanic Scholarship Fund
- March of Dimes
- Give the Kids the World
- Jackie Robinson Foundation
- Leadership Education for Asian Pacifics
- Asian American Scholarship Fund
- Junior Achievement

Each year Anheuser-Busch contributes millions of dollars to various organizations as part of its "Concern for People, Communities, and the Environment—A Way of Life" commitment.

Chick-fil-A

"We exist to glorify God by being a faithful steward of all that is entrusted to us and to have a positive influence on all who come in contact with Chick-fil-A."

(from Chick-fil-A's Official Statement of Corporate Purpose)

Truett Cathy founded Chick-fil-A more than 50 years ago in a small Georgia town. What began as a small, single restaurant has grown into one of the largest privately held restaurant chains in the nation. In 2000, the Chick-fil-A company reached $1 billion in sales. Part of its success has been due to the invention of the boneless chicken sandwich, an idea Cathy had many years ago which has spread widely since.

When the company began, they only operated stores in malls. Because Cathy believes that "every employee and restaurant operator should have the opportunity to worship, spend time with family and friends, or just plain rest from the workweek," every Chick-fil-A restaurant is closed on Sundays. When a Chick-fil-A restaurant within a mall is closed, the company incurs fines for every day that it is closed, because as part of each contract the stores within a mall must operate when the mall is open or pay a fee.

Chick-fil-A has enjoyed success in both business and society. The company is involved in many areas, such as investing in scholarships, character-building programs for children, and foster homes. Cathy began his mission to help children and develop future leaders more than 50 years ago, and this mission has flourished into the WinShape Centre Foundation. This foundation includes programs such as the WinShape Centre Foundation Scholarship Program at Berry College, Camp WinShape for Boys, Camp WinShape for Girls, and WinShape homes. Chick-fil-A also hosts the Chick-fil-A Charity Championship, a golf tournament, and has sponsored the Peach Bowl, an annual football game held in Atlanta, Georgia.

The activities of Chick-fil-A's charitable enterprise include the following:

• **WinShape Centre Scholarship Program.** This is a cooperative program that Chick-fil-A runs with Berry College, which is located in Rome, Georgia. The Centre offers four-year scholarships to incoming first-year students from around the nation who desire to attend this college.

• **Camp WinShape.** Camp sessions are two weeks in duration. During this time, boys and girls participate in activities such as rock climbing, archery, backpacking, canoeing, and a ropes course. Each year more than 1,500 campers from 22 states and two foreign countries attend camp at Berry College. This program was established in order to encourage youth and to help "shape winners," and it is based on the premise that "It is better to build boys than to mend men."

- **WinShape Homes.** This program was created to provide long-term foster care for children who are in need of a caring family environment. It was intended to provide a chance for children to "become all they can and desire to be." Each home contains two full-time, paid parents and up to 12 children. As opposed to the typical foster care program, which requires children to leave the home at age 18, this program encourages children to consider their foster home as their permanent home. The program and parents also encourage the children to attend college and to return to the home on weekends and vacations.

- **Chick-fil-A Charity Championship.** This event is held at the Eagle's Landing Country Club in Atlanta, Georgia, and is hosted by Nancy Lopez. It brings together many corporate sponsors and volunteers. It also draws the world's top players and more than 100,000 spectators. All proceeds from this event are donated to WinShape Homes and Adventures in Movement (AIM) for the Handicapped.

- **The Chick-fil-A Peach Bowl.** This event is an annual college football matchup held in Atlanta, Georgia, between Atlantic Coast Conference (ACC) and Southeastern Conference (SEC) teams. This sponsorship provides millions of dollars of proceeds to the participating universities and benefits the Chick-fil-A company, which operates many of its stores in ACC and SEC territories.

Chick-fil-A is very dedicated to the support and advancement of society. Truett Cathy has set a high standard with regard to the encouragement of children and the furthering of community-based programs.

Coca-Cola Company

"The Coca-Cola Company exists to benefit and refresh everyone who is touched by our business."

(The Coca-Cola Promise)

Owners of perhaps the world's most recognized brand and symbol, the Coca-Cola Company has a long and storied history of community involvement and outreach. Since its founding in 1886 by Dr. John Pemberton, the inventor of the beverage, Coca-Cola has played a leadership role in community, regional, national, and worldwide programs and activities. Headquartered in Atlanta, Georgia, and working through a distribution system of bottling companies, Coca-Cola can be found in more than 200 countries and territories around the world. Now the producers of numerous beverages, some of which are unavailable in the United States, it is estimated that 13,000 Coca-Cola products are consumed every *second* of the day.

In 1984, the company established the Coca-Cola Foundation to address many of its philanthropic interests. The company has established continent-specific foundations in Europe, Asia, Africa, and the Americas. The following is a partial list of the programs Coca-Cola supports and participates in, either singly or in conjunction with other organizations.

EDUCATION

- Adopt-a-School in Pakistan
- Building Schools in Ecuador
- Coca-Cola Educational Venture in the Philippines
- Coca-Cola Scholars Foundation
- Coca-Cola Valued Youth
- Critical Differences for Women
- E-Learning in Asia and Beyond
- First Generation Scholars
- Hope for the Young in Indonesia
- Little Red Schoolhouse
- Mexican School Shelters
- Moscow Education Committee Partnership
- New Zealand's Starship Children's Hospital Program
- National Museum Fellows Program
- Project Hope
- Upromise
- Youth Partnerships

ENVIRONMENT

Beijing Tree Planting Initiative

El Salvador Tree Planting Initiative

Rivers Alive

Greenhouse Challenge Cuts Energy Use

Argentina: Playful Environmental Program for Pre-teens

Lebanon CedaRoots Project

Italian National Recycling Day

National Park Discovery Center

Recycling with Scouts in the Philippines

Columbia Cleanup Day

Inspia! Leaders Who Inspire Action

SPONSORSHIPS

Art of Harmony

Boys and Girls Clubs of America

Children's Miracle Network

FIFA

NASCAR

International Olympics

Tiger Woods Foundation

HEALTH

Africa HIV/AIDS Programs (sponsored by the Coca-Cola Africa Foundation)

C onAgra Foods, Inc.

"Through leadership partnerships and financial contributions, ConAgra Foods is committed to improving the quality of life in communities across America."

(ConAgra Foods Leadership Initiative Statement)

ConAgra Foods is one of North America's largest food companies, with a strong presence in the consumer grocery, restaurant, and food service industries. Among ConAgra's several recognizable brands are Butterball, Banquet, Hunt's, Blue Bonnet, Chef Boyardee, and Chun King.

The focus of the Company's community leadership initiatives centers on two elements: feeding children better and home food safety.

The Feeding Children Better initiative addresses three areas:

1. Safe Havens funds KIDS CAFES, which are safe havens that provide nourishing meals and snacks as well as after school mentoring. This program is operated in conjunction with America's Second Harvest and numbers 85 KIDS CAFES in communities across the country.

2. Putting Food in Pantries funds the Rapid Food Distribution System, a computerized inventory and tracking system that is able to deliver food more quickly and efficiently to food banks that distribute food to hungry families and children. The company is donating approximately 100 trucks to food banks in the United States.

3. Raising Awareness is a company-supported effort in collaboration with America's Second Harvest and the Ad Council that created a multi-media campaign concerning child hunger. The campaign has run continuously since 2001.

In the Home Food Safety initiative, ConAgra joined with the American Dietetic Association to promote the publication "Home Food Safety . . . It's in Your Hands" The program is designed to educate all people about the essentials of food safety practices in their homes, especially the very young and older Americans with vulnerable immune systems. The program is built around four simple messages:

- Wash your hands often.
- Keep raw meats and ready-to-eat foods separate.
- Cook food to proper temperatures.
- Refrigerate foods properly below 40 degrees Fahrenheit.

The ConAgra Foods Foundation has had a long-term alliance with America's Second Harvest. The company is an original founding member of the American Red Cross Annual Disaster Giving Program, which provides food to people in communities in need of disaster relief.

The firm also provides funding for minority students to reach their educational goals. Recipients of funds include Consortium for Graduate Study in Management, the American Indian College Fund, and the United Negro College Fund.

The company strongly supports the Montfort Children's Clinic in Greeley, Colorado, which assists children and pregnant women in need of counseling and medical attention.

ConAgra Foods Foundation is a major supporter of Underground Adventure at Chicago's Field Museum which raises awareness of the ecosystem in areas where crops and plants grow.

The company honored its milling heritage by contributing to the STUHR Museum in Grand Island, Nebraska, and the Minnesota Historical Society, both of which operate flour mill exhibits.

The firm has a strong commitment to environmental issues in the areas of water, air, energy, and land. They have formed the Sustainable Development Council to oversee environmental matters and provide recognition and awards to those who achieve marked success with environmental projects. Thirteen ConAgra food plants earned charter membership in the

National Environmental Achievement Track, an honor bestowed by the Environmental Protection Agency (EPA).

D arden Restaurants

"We believe community involvement is part of our civic rent. When guests dine in our restaurants, they are buying more than a great meal, they are also 'buying' our ethics. It's the way you do business when you intend to be the best company in the casual dining industry, now and for generations."

(Joe R. Lee, chairman and CEO)

Darden is the largest casual dining company in the world. Headquartered in Orlando, Florida, the company owns and operates five brands: Red Lobster, Olive Garden, Bahama Breeze, Smokey Bones, and Seasons 52. It also operates the Darden Environmental Trust and the Darden Foundation.

Under the Darden Environmental Trust, the Red Lobster Partners in Preservation program, founded in 1992, has worked to clean up lakes, rivers, and beaches throughout North America. Red Lobster employees dedicate several days each year to these environmental projects and have collected hundreds of tons of litter and harmful refuse, making our waterways and beaches safer and cleaner.

The Darden Environmental Trust works with the World Conservation Trust Foundation to help preserve, protect, and improve the environment while still providing food for the growing world population. Trust representatives visit Darden supply organizations throughout the world, ensuring that suppliers' practices are responsible in terms of environmental protection. The Trust is also involved in a project that protects the Kemps Ridley sea turtle, the most endangered sea turtle in the world, as well as the nesting spots of loggerhead and leatherback turtles.

The Darden Foundation focuses its attention on social services, nutrition, arts and culture, education, and the preservation of natural resources. It also provides resources to programs in which its employees and retirees are involved and has a keen interest in supporting programs that promote diversity, inclusiveness, and fairness.

Here is a representative sample of the types of programs the Darden Foundation supports:

ARTS AND CULTURE

- Atlantic Center for the Arts
- Southern Ballet Theater

- MichLee Puppets
- Orlando Museum of Arts
- Jack Kerouac Writers in Residence

EDUCATION

- Adult Literacy League, Inc.
- HiTech Tutoring Center
- National Urban League
- Holocaust Memorial Resource and Education Center
- Numerous colleges and universities

SOCIAL SERVICES

- American Red Cross
- Canine Companion for Independence
- Meals on Wheels, Inc.
- Living Hope International, Inc.
- Mustard Seed, Inc.

NATIONAL RESOURCES

- Horseshoe Creek Wildlife Foundation
- The Lobster Conservancy
- National Resources Foundation of Wisconsin
- Valley Zoological Foundation
- Central Florida Zoological Society, Inc.

The larger Darden Restaurants brands also have special charitable promotions. Red Lobster has an annual Cops and Lobsters Day in which law enforcement officials act as celebrity servers with the proceeds of the day's sales being donated to the International Special Olympics.

Olive Garden has a Pasta for Pennies program that invites school children to collect pennies for the Leukemia and Lymphoma Society of America. School classes compete against each other, and the class that raises the most funds receives a catered lunch from Olive Garden.

The breadth and depth of what the Darden organization supports is not well known, except by the recipients of its largesse. They are truly institutional leaders in their communities.

D uPont

"DuPont is committed to improving the quality of life and enhancing the vitality of the communities in which it operates throughout the world."

(excerpt from the DuPont Philosophy)

Delaware-based DuPont is a company delivering science-based solutions in markets such as food and nutrition, health care, apparel, home and construction, electronics, and transportation. They operate in 70 countries worldwide, and approximately half of their 80,000 employees work outside the United States.

In the field of education, DuPont's mission is to sustain the "miracles of science" by nurturing global collaborative research and education. To that end, the company initiated the following:

1. The Center for Collaborative Research & Education (CCRE) facilitates partnerships, scholarships, and grants to universities and government laboratories worldwide. Numerous universities and institutes receive funds to ensure and improve science literacy, workforce preparation, and business and community sustainability.

2. Higher Education Partnerships, initiated in 1918, awarded scholarships and fellowships at 48 U.S. colleges and universities. The program has expanded to more than 200 colleges and universities worldwide. The partnerships operate at both the graduate and undergraduate levels, with many initiatives focusing on increased participation of underrepresented populations.

3. The DuPont Office of Education (DOE) works with leading educators and local business leaders to prepare today's children for tomorrow's world. The initiatives include:

   • bringing inquiry-based science programs to communities where DuPont operates,

   • nurturing young Americans' interest in science and mathematics through national and international competitions,

   • encouraging underrepresented minorities to consider careers in science and mathematics,

   • safeguarding the competence of teachers of science and mathematics.

In addition to education, DuPont also strongly supports the arts and culture, environmental initiatives, human and health service organizations, and community and civic activities. Two programs are the core of their corporate effort in this regard.

1. The *DuPont Community Fund* has provided support to more than 400 projects worldwide in the past 14 years. The fund matches 100 percent, up to $10,000, of the donations made by DuPont plants and offices for programs that benefit community life. The company's sites nominate projects for *DuPont Community Fund* consideration and awards are granted on an annual basis.

2. The DuPont Volunteer Recognition awards program acknowledges the volunteer efforts of company employees who donate their time and talents to improving the quality of life in their communities. Employees who are honored receive recognition, and $1,000 grants are awarded to the organization for which the employees provide their volunteer service.

E astman Kodak

"Eastman Kodak Company has an active community relations and contributions program designed to support the achievement of company goals."
(excerpt from the Community Relations and Contributions Statement)

The first Kodak camera was introduced to the consumer in 1888. The company's founder, George Eastman, began his journey into the world of photography in 1879, when he travelled to London, England, the "center of the photographic world." It was during the following year that he began commercially manufacturing dry plates, which led to his partnership with Henry A. Strong. The partnership resulted in the opening of the Eastman Dry Plate Company in January of 1881.

In 1883 Eastman introduced his latest invention, film in rolls and a roll holder that was adaptable to almost every plate camera. In 1884, a new firm was created, the Eastman Dry Plate and Film Company. In 1889, after the release of the Kodak camera, the Eastman Company was formed. This company was renamed the Eastman Kodak Company in 1892, and this name has been extant for more than 100 years.

The first Kodak camera was preloaded with enough film for 100 exposures and it could be hand held during operation. For development, the entire camera was returned, the prints were made, and the camera was reloaded. Over the years Eastman continued to innovate and progressively simplify photography. Today, Eastman Kodak Company has operations and manufacturing plants in more than 150 countries and is one of the most widely recognized symbols in the world of photography.

In Eastman's early years he enjoyed music and "firmly believed that the progress of the world depends almost entirely on education." Due to this belief, Eastman and the Eastman Kodak Company have generously given to organizations in this area. The University of Rochester has been a large beneficiary of these efforts, housing the Eastman School of Music and the Eastman Theatre, which is the home of the Rochester Philharmonic Orchestra.

Eastman's philanthropy, considered a part of life and business, has been far reaching. Eastman began his efforts when making only $60 a week, by donating funds to the Mechanics Institute of Rochester, which was young and struggling to stay afloat. He also donated money to the Massachusetts Institute of Technology (MIT) after hiring some of its graduates, who became some of his best assistants. His donation to MIT was anonymous, made under the name of Mr. Smith.

Other areas Eastman viewed as important, and, in turn, to which he contributed to were hospitals and dental clinics. He produced the plans and funds for the creation of a dental clinic in Rochester, New York, and later clinics were built in London, Paris, Rome, Brussels, and Stockholm. After studying the field of medicine, Eastman helped the University of Rochester form a medical school and hospital.

In one day during 1924, Eastman donated $30 million to the University of Rochester, MIT, Hampton, and Tuskegee. He explained these huge donations to a selected few in a statement: "I selected a limited number of recipients because I wanted to cover certain kinds of education and felt I could get results with those named quicker and more directly than if the money were spread."

Eastman's philanthropic efforts also can be seen in his business practices and developments. His employees greatly benefited from these efforts, which included the development of the Wage Dividend Program and the creation of retirement annuity, life insurance, and disability benefit plans. In 1899, Eastman distributed to his employees a large amount of his own money, which was an "outright gift" to them. The Wage Dividend program benefited each employee in proportion to the yearly dividend on the company stock. In 1919, Eastman gave away one-third of his own company stock to his employees. He felt the prosperity of an organization was highly correlated to workers' goodwill and loyalty, which were enhanced by forms of profit sharing. He saw employee dedication as more pertinent to prosperity than inventions and patents.

Today, Eastman Kodak supports many initiatives and contributes to many different programs related to these areas. A few examples in each of these areas are as follows:

PROGRAMS

- Campaign to Encourage Minority Parents' Involvement in Public Schools
- Shelters for homeless women
- National Health Museum
- Urban Revitalization Plan—Rochester, New York

DIVERSITY

- National Museum of African Arts
- Scholarships to minority students
- Hispanic American history supplements
- Supplier diversity

VOLUNTEERS

- Habitat for Humanity
- Kudos to Kodak
- Agentina da la mano a su comunidad
- Local community cleanups

The Eastman Kodak Company has been very generous to its employees and the community over the past 100-odd years. The company has aided in areas that it felt were important to the company and its employees. The focused efforts, donations, and volunteer hours have been in areas that "instill employee pride, build public trust, foster education, respond to community needs, and enhance company image."

ord Motor Company

"As we endeavor to become a leading contributor to a more sustainable world, corporate citizenship has become an integral part of every decision and action we take."
(excerpt from the Corporate Citizenship preamble of the Ford Motor Company)

Ford Motor Company, which is based in Dearborn, Michigan, is one of the most recognized names in the world. Henry Ford, the inventor of the "horseless carriage" is an indelible icon in the annals of world business history. The company he founded has a checkered past with respect to its profitability, but in recent times it has prospered (relatively) and invests in corporate citizenship in a significant way.

It is important to note that the Ford Foundation is a separate entity quite removed from the automobile manufacturer. Although the initial funding for the Ford Foundation was seeded by Henry Ford and others, no member of the Ford family or Ford's management currently sits on the foundation's board of directors. Although the foundation is worthy of recognition in its own right, this profile focuses instead on the company.

The company manages the Ford Motor Company Fund, which supports initiatives in five areas: (1) education, (2) environment, (3) public policy, (4) civic affairs and community development, and (5) and the arts and humanities.

1. Education Through the College Relations Sponsor Program (CRSP), the fund has donated millions of dollars to 31 CRSP schools, including five historically black colleges and universities and one all-female institution. One of the recipients is the University of Michigan's Center for the Education of Women, where the fund supports 10 Ford Fellowships.

Other endeavors of the Ford Motor Company in the area of education include:

- Future Farmers of America (FFA)—scholarships for aspiring students
- United Negro College Fund—scholarships
- The Hispanic Scholarship Fund—scholarships
- American Indian College Fund—scholarships
- Golden Key National Honor Society—scholarships
- International Fellowship Program
- Ford Detroit Free Press High School Foundation Program
- Henry Ford Academy—a charter school
- Jobs for America's Graduates (JAG)
- Detroit Lions Academy—middle school programs
- Ford Academy of Manufacturing Sciences (FAMS)

2. Environment The company is a partner in the jointly sponsored Proud Partner Program in conjunction with the National Park Foundation, the U.S. National Park Service, and private industry. This program was designed to help manage congestion, promote sustainability, and meet other transportation and environmental needs. The program also includes the Ford Proud Partner Transportation Interpreter Program, wherein national park interns provide interpretive services that enhance the visitor experience on alternative transportation vehicles in the parks.

Other environmental programs include support for:
a. Conservation International—protects biologically diverse areas
b. Center for Environmental Leadership—works to conserve water in manufacturing
c. Wildlife Habitat Council—preservation of natural environments
d. Environmental Career Organization—internships targeted at helping the industry reduce its impact on the environment
e. Princeton Carbon Mitigation Initiative—program to reduce the impact of carbon and greenhouse gas emissions

f. Chicago Environmental Fund—works to sustain the ecology of Chicago's Calumet region

g. Earthwatch Institute—supports conservation research in North and South America, Asia, and Africa

h. Support of city zoos in Detroit, Michigan; Kansas City, Missouri; and Atlanta, Georgia, as well as other cities

3. Public Policy, Health and Social Programs The Ford Motor Company Fund provides a grant to Promise Stations, an online resource for at-risk youth available in 600 communities throughout the nation at no charge. The Promise Stations bring together community resources for at-risk youth so that they can experience the five promises of the program: (1) caring adults, (2) safe places, (3) a healthy start, (4) marketable skills, and (5) opportunities to serve.

In addition, the company supported the following programs in the public policy, health, and social programs sector:

- Disabled American Veterans scholarship program
- Multiple United Way campaigns
- Robin Hood Foundation—relief for the September 11, 2001, tragedy
- Chefs Across America—relief for the September 11, 2001, tragedy
- Boost America Campaigns—free booster seats for 4–8-year-old children of needy families
- Bowling for Burns Tournament—support for burn prevention and treatment programs
- Future Cities Competition—invites middle school students to create the cities of tomorrow
- Christina's Smile—provides dental care for children in need

4. Civic Affairs and Community Development The company provides financial support for a plethora of civic and community programs which include:

- National Hispanic Leadership Institute
- National Conference for Community and Justice
- National Latino Elected and Appointed Officials (NALEO) Education Fund
- National Council of Negro Women
- The Hope Fund
- Americans for Indian Opportunity
- Japanese American Citizens League
- Vista Maria

- Arab American Chamber of Commerce
- Jewish Federation of Metropolitan Detroit

5. Arts and Humanities A long-time benefactor of the arts and humanities, the Ford Motor Company Fund sponsors several museum exhibitions including:

- Half Past Autumn: The Art of Gordon Parks
- Norman Rockwell: Pictures for the American People
- British Museum Ford Centre for Young Visitors
- Albert Kahn: Inspiration for the Modern
- To Conserve a Legacy: American Art from Historically Black Colleges and Universities

The performing arts also are recipients of the firm's support. Among other programs supported are the following:

- University Musical Society at the University of Michigan—featured Marcel Marceau
- Playwrights Horizon—off-Broadway theater renovation, expansion, and community outreach
- Ford Community and Performing Arts Center
- Ford Motor Company Research Institute for Women in Jazz, in conjunction with the American Jazz Museum in Kansas City
- Silk Road Project—led by cellist Yo-Yo Ma, a team of international scholars, museums, and artists providing concerts and festivals throughout the world

ershey Foods Corporation

"Hershey Foods Corporation is committed to being a good neighbor and improving quality of community life."

(excerpt from the Corporate Contributions Statement)

As a leading manufacturer of quality chocolate and nonchocolate confectionary items and chocolate-related grocery store products, Hershey Foods Corporation sells many different products domestically and maintains a variety of international operations.

In 1876, Milton Hershey gave the candy business a try. He opened a business in Philadelphia that failed after six years. He tried and failed at many other operations over the coming years. In 1886, Hershey finally established himself as a candy maker with the opening of his business, the Lancaster Caramel Company. In 1894, the Hershey Chocolate Company was created as a subsidiary of the Lancaster Caramel Company. Six years later, Mr. Hershey sold the caramel business but retained the chocolate manufacturing equipment. He moved back to his hometown of Derry Church, Pennsylvania, and in 1903 proceeded to establish and grow what is now the largest chocolate manufacturing plant and one of the most well-known chocolate companies in North America.

Through his many endeavors at breaking into the candy business, Hershey found that the key to a superior product was the use of fresh milk. It was in the town of Derry Church that he found an ample supply to mass-produce his staple product, milk chocolate. It was also in this small town that Milton Hershey established a community that was built around the manufacturing plant.

In this community, Mr. Hershey and his wife began the most personally important of his philanthropic efforts, the Milton Hershey School. This school continues to provide education for approximately 1,100 children whose lives have been disrupted in some way. The school is funded by the Hershey Trust Company, which was also established by Mr. Hershey within this community.

Hershey Foods also supports many other areas of the community through both cash and product contributions, including health and human services, civic and community initiatives, arts and culture, and the environment. The company especially focuses its efforts in those communities where many of its employees reside or where its plants are located.

Hershey's main program within the community is the Hershey's Track and Field Youth Program. It is the largest youth sports program of its kind in North America. This program is aimed at children ages 9–14 and is focused on introducing these children to physical fitness through basic track and field events. This program is also sponsored by the President's Council of Physical Fitness and Sports, the National Recreation Association, and the National Association for Sport and Physical Education.

ewlett-Packard

"Good citizenship is good business. We live up to our responsibility to society by being an economic, intellectual, and social asset to each country and community in which we do business."
(excerpt from the Global Citizenship Statement)

Established in 1939 by two Stanford University engineering graduates, Hewlett-Packard (HP) has grown from a single product developed in a garage in Palo Alto, California, to a leader in its industry.

The company merged with Compaq Computer Corporation in May, 2002, and is now referred to as the "new HP." The new corporation is lead by

Carly Fiorina, the company's chairperson and CEO. Its headquarters are still located in Palo Alto. The company consists of four core business groups: Enterprise Systems Group, Imaging and Printing Group, HP Services, and Personal Systems Group. These groups are based on seven corporate objectives that were instituted for the new HP: customer loyalty, profit, market leadership, growth, employee commitment, leadership capability, and global citizenship.

It is in this final corporate objective that HP's commitment to society can be evidenced. The corporation's philanthropic efforts are recognized throughout the globe. In order to be an exemplary corporate global citizen, the company contributes funds and volunteer hours to causes such as diversity, inclusion, and work/life navigation, and it models its behavior and practices to help bridge the digital divide. The areas that the company views as important to bridging this divide are corporate governance, environmental policies and practices, community engagement, and e-inclusion (educating people in the electronic age).

HP also runs an invent sponsorship program. This program promotes pushing the boundaries of invention and creativity, and it is a way for the company to celebrate talent and innovation in the fields of art and creativity. Examples of sponsorships are the Young Inventors Contest and the Ansel Adams at 100 Exhibition.

The e-inclusion program is unique and was created to aid and allow all people to use technology as a means to learn, work, and thrive in society. This program creates new market opportunities and seeks to close the gap between "technology-empowered and technology-excluded communities."

Environmentally, HP sees a need to reduce its footprint on the environment, as well as those of its customers and partners. It believes that by developing products and solutions that reduce the company's effect on the environment, it will be able to lead the way to sustainable business.

HP's philanthropic efforts and its commitment to the communities in which it serves can be traced as far back as the inception of the company in 1939.

---

ilton Hotels

"There is a natural law, a Divine law, that obliges you and me to relieve the suffering, the distressed, the destitute. Charity is a supreme virtue and the great channel through which the mercy of God is passed on to mankind. It is that virtue that unites men and inspires their noblest efforts."

(excerpt from the Last Will and Testament of Conrad Nicholson Hilton)

Hilton Hotels has more than 500 properties worldwide and encompasses eight brands. The founder, Conrad N. Hilton, bought his first hotel in 1919 in

Cisco, Texas, and developed the company into an internationally recognized brand until his death in 1979. One of Conrad's sons, Barron, is now chairperson of the company's board of directors. The company plays a leadership role in the communities in which it operates by participating in local promotions, charities, sponsored events, and in-kind services. Hilton employees are active volunteers in many community organizations.

These activities are conducted through two separate entities: the Hilton Foundation, founded by Conrad Hilton in 1944, and the Conrad N. Hilton Fund (CNHF), which also supports various programmatic interests. These two entities, plus related funds, total approximately $1.7 billion in assets. The foundation and the fund support multiple causes, a partial listing of which follows:

- The Perkins School for the Blind—is devoted to educating deaf, blind, and multi-handicapped children in the United States, Latin America, and India.

- The Carter Center, World Vision, Helen Keller International—an organization working to prevent and control the spread of trachoma, the leading cause of blindness throughout the world. Programs exist in the developing countries of Africa, Asia, and other locations around the globe.

- Ghana Rural Water Project—is devoted to eradicating the Guinea worm, which adversely affects populations through contaminated water and poor sanitation facilities. (The effort to eradicate the Guinea worm extends beyond the nation of Ghana.)

- Mexico's Water Forever Program—is operated in conjunction with the Ford Foundation and local resources.

- Water for People—addresses the issue of arsenic contamination in water.

- Cornell International Institute on Food, Agriculture and Development—supports sustainable agriculture in countries around the world.

- Originated and continues to support the Conrad N. Hilton College of Hotel and Restaurant Management at the University of Houston.

- Culinary Institute of America—supports the library that houses the world's largest collection of culinary books and videos.

- Annually funds 40 "Hilton Scholars" with scholarships administered through the American Hotel and Lodging Association's Foundation.

- Family Violence Prevention Fund (developed by the National Health Initiative on Domestic Violence)—is devoted to training care providers to recognize signs of abuse and how to intervene effectively.

- Center for Prevention of Sexual and Domestic Violence—an interfaith organization that educates clergy, lay leaders, denominational staff, and seminary faculty in matters relating to counseling clients in crisis.

- Corporation for Supportive Housing for its Closer to Home initiative—supports programs that stabilize street dwellers, long-term emergency shelter residents, and other mentally ill homeless people.
- Early Head Start (EHS) programs—supports infants and toddlers with disabilities and trains staff to work with them.
- Project ALERT—a two-year drug prevention curriculum for middle grade students.
- Roman Catholic Sisters—primarily supports programs in the human services field.

In 1996, the foundation established the Conrad N. Hilton Humanitarian Prize, a cash award of $1 million recognizing a charitable or non-governmental organization that makes extraordinary contributions to alleviating human suffering anywhere in the world. Past recipients have been:

- Operation Smile
- International Rescue Committee
- Doctors Without Borders
- African Medical and Research Foundation
- Casa Alianza
- St. Christopher's Hospice
- SOS-Kinderdorf International

yatt Corporation

"Inherent with the company's philosophy is the goal to give back to the local community and environment wherever and whenever it can."

(Hyatt's Company Overview—Social Consciousness)

Headquartered in Chicago, Illinois, Hyatt Hotels is a privately held corporation owned by the Pritzker family. They operate more than 200 hotels and resorts managed by two separate groups of companies, Hyatt International Corporation and Hyatt Hotels Corporation.

While Hyatt Regency Hotels is the firm's primary brand, it also has in its portfolio the upscale, luxurious Grand Hyatt brand and the smaller Park Hyatt, which suggests a European influence.

Each Hyatt property and satellite office contributes to community and environmental activities through the company's Family of Responsible and Caring Employees (F.O.R.C.E.) program, and each management employee is allowed two paid workdays each year for volunteer work in the community. The company also participates in the following programs:

- The company has created environmental consciousness programs on a local, national, and worldwide scale, including recycling and the employee instruction of others on recycling needs and techniques.

- In 2000, the company developed a program it calls Focus 2000, which addresses diversity issues, training, and developmental needs for its workforce.

- Hyatt International has partnered with the Foundation for Small Voices, which raises funds in various communities to benefit children through concerts and musical workshops.

- Hyatt Hotels operates a scholarship program for minorities administered by the American Hotel & Lodging Association's Foundation. Hundreds of thousands of dollars have been awarded to qualified students over the past several years. The Pritzker family members have also been generous benefactors to the arts, museums, music, and architectural programs.

 # BM

"Good philanthropy is good business. . . ."

(IBM Commitment to Corporate Citizenship)

IBM (originally International Business Machines), based in Armonk, New York, is one of the largest international organizational solutions companies in the world. Widely and affectionately known as "Big Blue," the company has long enjoyed the status of a worldwide leading computer company.

Since its inception, IBM has placed great emphasis on community relations and contributes to various programs, universities, projects, and charities throughout the world. The following is a sampling:

- Reinventing Education—provides funds to support higher quality training for U.S. public school teachers. IBM has been granted the Leader for Change Award for Sustained Excellence by the Council for Aid to Education for the support of this program.

- Kidsmart Early Learning—provides grants to assist children in early developmental stages to begin learning. It also initiated a new Web site for parents and teachers, which provides guidance in early learning and technology.

- Provides handheld computing devices that represent the next generation of assistive technology for museums to support Egyptian Museum visitors.

- IBM MentorPlace—a volunteer program that allows thousands of IBM personnel around the globe to provide students with academic assistance and career counseling.

- EXCITE CAMPS—supports 600 sixth and seventh grade girls in attending summer camp.

- Swirl Project—using IBM-donated technology, Victoria University of Technology School of Education (Australia) students are providing literacy and computer skills to Aboriginal students through Story Writing in Remote Locations (SWIRL).

- National Science and Teaching Center for Australia—donated funds and technology to refurbish "Mathematica," an interactive exhibit that teaches math concepts to children and adults.

- South Africa Education Improvement Projects—provides services and technology focused on primary, secondary, and tertiary education.

- Established the Women's Computer Training Center in Bosnia.

- Gandhi Institute of Computer Education and Information Technology— helps provide IT training for students from economically disadvantaged backgrounds in India.

- The Solutions Network—connects welfare recipients with gainful employment and links businesses with welfare-to-work resources in their communities.

- Adult Literacy Partnership—in collaboration with seven nonprofit literacy groups, IBM researchers are developing education and special needs software to help adults improve their literacy skills.

- State Hermitage Museum (Russia)—developed a digital library of high-resolution masterpieces, a first-of-its-kind Web site, and an Image Creation Studio which makes it possible to view the museum's great treasures through the Internet.

- TryScience—the first on-line worldwide science and technology center featuring interactive exhibits, multimedia adventures, live field trips, and hands-on science projects.

- Donated a computer to enrich Bangkok's Thailand Educational Science Center, where visitors learn about technology.

- Teaming for Technology—working with other social service organizations, this program is designed to enhance technology skills and maximize the effectiveness of social service agencies.

- The Used Technology Donation Program—working with Gifts in Kind International, this program donates used personal computer systems to nonprofit organizations that provide adult education and training.

- Canadian National Institute for the Blind—IBM Canadian Headquarters served as the host for the Gretzky SCORE (Summer Computer Opportunities in Recreation and Education) Teen Camp, which gave visually impaired and blind teens a chance to develop a positive sense of self and an opportunity to learn IT skills.

- IBM Matching Grants Programs—matches gifts made by employees and retirees to nonprofit organizations and educational institutions.

- Support of Education Summits—helped launch the European E-Learning Summit (2001) and cohosted the Latin America Basic Education Summit (2002).

For these and numerous other initiatives, IBM twice has been named the Best Corporate Citizen, according to *Business Ethics* Corporate Social Responsibility Report.

Intel

"By ensuring that today's children have access to the resources, skills, and experiences they need, Intel's goal is to provide a foundation so that students can become effective leaders in the future."

(excerpt from Intel in Your Community)

In 1971, Intel introduced the world's first microprocessor. Since then Intel has continued to pioneer the business of computer technology. It has helped change the way the world utilizes information and communicates across all distances and boundaries. What was originally founded as a semiconductor memory product company in 1968 has grown to be one of the world's most prominent producers of chips, boards, systems, and software building blocks. These products are the components that make up computers, servers, and networking and communications products.

Intel is defined by three main categories of products and services: PCs and enterprise systems, networking and communications, and wireless communications and computing. The company currently operates 12 fabrication facilities and 12 assembly and test facilities around the world, and it is striving to become a 100 percent e-corporation in the future. In order to continue in its leadership role, Intel heavily invests in research and development because technology is a business of continuous change. Without the ability to envision what comes next or what could be next, it would be easy to fall behind.

Intel has a history of philanthropy in the communities that it serves, and its generosity is evident worldwide. Intel's giving, however, is very focused so that it might achieve the best results possible. The majority of the company's donations are in the areas of math and science education and technology literacy programs. Distributions are in the form of donations, sponsorships, and grants.

One such program is called the Intel Model School Program. This program promotes technology use in the classroom by making sure that school districts have the tools and resources they need. The program establishes links between the school districts and hardware vendors, software developers, and service providers. There are other programs that Intel has recently supported in certain locales: education Web sites, sculpture for children, and various international campaigns.

EDUCATIONAL WEB SITES

The educational Web site Investigate Biodiversity was created in 2001 in partnership with Conservation International. It allows high school students to follow the investigation of scientists studying exotic ecoresearch. It was created with the hope that some of these young people might one day give back to their communities by coming up with innovative ideas on how to "protect regions rich in animal and plant life."

Intel has also created, in collaboration with the Nature Conservancy, a Web site aimed at middle school students. This Web site, Last Great Places, allows children to view preserved places that are unique, natural areas. These places are located in the United States, Latin America, the Caribbean, and the Pacific.

SCULPTURE FOR CHILDREN

This program was created for children who suffer from behavioral and emotional problems at the B'nai B'rith Home in Israel. The focus is on helping children to understand the importance of environmental preservation.

INTERNATIONAL CAMPAIGNS

Ireland—Intel's sites in Ireland are very active within their communities. One of their projects has been a partnership with a local school in an aluminum can recycling effort. They also have helped plant trees, plants, and shrubs to beautify the land and increase the local butterfly populations.

Philippines—These Intel sites and their employees have been active in the Philippine communities on many different levels. A few of these efforts include providing free medical and dental services to residents of neighboring communities, conducting safety and health campaigns, contributing to local traffic safety, and educating teachers and students on safety and environmental issues.

These are just a few samples of the efforts that Intel supports. Intel heavily supports the preservation of the environment and seeks to educate the public. A large amount of support comes through the volunteer work of Intel's own employees, which is a testament to their determination.

Johnson & Johnson

"Through our contributions efforts, we are actively involved in supporting ongoing health care, educational, and cultural programs."

(excerpt from In the Community Statement)

Founded in 1886 by the Johnson brothers in a small building in New Brunswick, New Jersey, today Johnson & Johnson (J & J) is the "world's most comprehensive and broadly based manufacturer of health care products and provider of related services." J & J provides products and services to consumer, pharmaceutical, and professional markets. The organization currently includes 198 entities operating in more than 175 countries.

Johnson & Johnson's first president, Robert Wood Johnson, envisioned this company after hearing Sir Joseph Lister speak in 1876. Lister was an English surgeon who found that airborne germs were a source of infection in the operating room. Prior to his discovery, the postoperative mortality rate was approximately 90 percent in some hospitals. Johnson & Johnson began searching for the greatly needed solution to this devastating problem.

In 1887, Johnson & Johnson entered the surgical dressings industry, and in 1888 it published the book, *Modern Methods of Antiseptic Wound Treatment*, which was the standard text for antiseptic practices for many years. Over the next 31 years, the company continued to advance the surgical dressing industry with the invention of a new sterilization process and development of new products. In 1919, the company began to expand internationally and has continued its growth ever since.

Under the direction of Robert Wood Johnson, Jr., Johnson & Johnson took on a new corporate structure. This new structure was one of decentralization, which allowed the divisions and affiliates to chart their own paths. They were organized as individual divisions or subsidiaries that had autonomy to act on their own. It is in this fashion that the company continued to grow, acquiring companies that fit the corporate strategy and divesting others that did not. Today, the corporation operates in many different sectors and is a major presence in all of them.

Johnson & Johnson's philanthropic efforts can be traced back to 1906, when it began providing disaster relief supplies to victims of the earthquake in San Francisco. J & J has continued to supply relief to victims of such disasters as earthquakes, fires, floods, tornadoes, hurricanes, and terrorism. It also has a contributions program that it views as a worldwide social responsibility effort. It has four areas of expertise, which it uses to align its philanthropic efforts.

Johnson & Johnson's main philanthropic forums are company contributions, the environment, health and safety, and women's health. Each will be briefly discussed with examples given.

COMPANY CONTRIBUTIONS

Contributions occur in the form of money, time, and supplies. **Signature programs** are those that "carry the Johnson & Johnson logo and reflect a long-term financial commitment between the company and the program." These programs are focused on four areas: access to health care, children's health, professional development, and education and community responsibility. A few examples of these programs are:

- J & J Community Health Care Program
- J & J School Nurse Fellowship Program
- Yale–J & J International Physicians Scholars Program
- J & J Bridge to Employment Program

Non-signature programs are those which "represent important efforts and significant investments in efforts to help the underserved." These programs are focused on areas of global and community interests such as the environment, emerging social issues, and critical local nonprofit organizations. Some areas covered by these programs include:

- disaster relief
- international contributions
- SAFE KIDS Worldwide
- the arts

ENVIRONMENT

Johnson & Johnson is committed to environmental issues in all of the communities in which it serves. The company strives for environmental excellence through many different efforts, to which each of its companies and all employees are committed in order to achieve "global sustainable growth." The following are just a few of J & J's areas of interest:

- conservation and land use
- energy
- product and process development—design for the environment
- water

HEALTH AND SAFETY

Johnson & Johnson has a vision to be the world leader in health and safety. It strives toward this goal in many ways, such as eliminating workplace illness and injuries, sharing its best practices and establishing safety as good business. It is through many initiatives that J & J has established programs in its companies and in communities worldwide. A few brief examples of these initiatives are:

- Drexel University
- Machine Safety
- National Safety Council Online First Aid Course
- Occupational Health and Safety Assesment Series

WOMEN'S HEALTH

Women's health has long been an area of focus for Johnson & Johnson. They have formed a partnership with the University of California–San Francisco that supports collaborative and innovative efforts aimed at improving access for women to health care products and services. J & J's companies make up the "largest and most diverse women's health care products portfolio of any company in the world." Because of this business interest, the company has formed many different partnerships and programs, including:

Partnerships

- Cancer Care, Inc.
- National Women's Health Resource Center, Inc.
- Society for Women's Health Research
- The Women's Museum: An Institute for the Future

Programs

- Periods 201
- Women's Community Health Leadership Program

Johnson & Johnson has a long history of philantropic efforts and plans to continue such efforts in the future. It is very focused on its four areas of expertise and is fully committed to these initiatives. As a large conglomerate of companies, it is united on all of these fronts. This allows it to maximize the amount of benefits and results on the companies and the communities which it serves.

 ellogg's

"To help people help themselves through the practical application of knowledge and resources to improve their quality of life and that of future generations."
(the mission statement of the W. K. Kellogg Foundation, Will Keith Kellogg, founder)

Founded and headquartered in Battle Creek, Michigan, Kellogg's is the world's leading producer of cereal and a leading producer of convenience foods. Kellogg's products can be found in the kitchens of millions of homes around the world, and the company is a leading supplier to the food service industry. Kellogg's produces its products in 19 countries around the globe and reaches 160 countries in the world.

The company's watchword is "Kellogg's Cares," and its overriding emphasis centers on the following three areas of giving:

- helping children and youth reach their full potential
- improving access to health and human services
- building stronger communities

HEALTH AND HUMAN SERVICES

- America's Second Harvest—a nationwide network of food banks making food available to needy children and families.
- Disaster Relief—provides food in times of calamity and natural disasters.
- Dream Flights—a program that provides critically ill children with plane rides over Chicago with Ernie Keebler, the elficon for Keebler products.
- Race for the Cure—supports the Susan G. Komen Breast Cancer Foundation.

COMMUNITY DEVELOPMENT

- Medical Education for South African Blacks (MESAB)—improves the quality of health care through increased training opportunities for healthcare professionals.
- National Council of LaRaza—an organization dedicated to serving the needs of Hispanic people.
- National Urban League—a community-based organization helping African-Americans secure economic self-reliance and civil rights.
- United Way—supports the campaigns where Kellogg facilities are located across the country.

Kellogg's also has an active employee volunteerism program. Some of these activities include:

- Day of Caring—headquarters' employees spend part of a day at non-profit agencies that are part of the United Way Campaign.
- Habitat for Humanity—employees assist in building homes around the country for families in need.

- HOSTS—each week employees in six cities across the nation take time off for the Help One Student To Succeed Program by providing one-on-one tutoring at local elementary schools.

Marriott International, Inc.

"'Spirit to serve our communities' reflects the genuine desire of our facilities and associates to give resources, time and energy to help make a difference in the lives of others and the communities we work and live in."

(drawn from the "culture" of Marriott Corporation)

Marriott International, based in Washington, D.C., is one of the world's foremost lodging companies with approximately 2,500 lodging properties located in all 50 states and 64 countries and territories. The company has 14 brands and operates in all segments of the lodging industry, as well as in vacation ownership resorts. The Marriott family also manages a family foundation called the J. Willard and Alice S. Marriott Foundation, which has contributed significantly to educational, medical, and cultural programs around the nation.

The company and foundation support and participate in numerous national and worldwide programs, among which are the following:

- America's Promise—helping at-risk high school youths transition to meaningful careers by providing financial assistance for education, internships, and job shadowing opportunities, with particular involvement in National Groundhog Job Shadow Day.

- Pathways to Independence—provides classroom and job-site training to economically disadvantaged and chronically unemployed individuals to overcome hurdles for job placement and retention.

- Marriott Foundation for People with Disabilities—a program operating in six major U.S. cities to provide "Bridges . . . from school to work" to high school graduates who have a disability, giving them access to productive and fulfilling work opportunities.

- Marriott Family Services Fund—supports organizations that address childcare, transportation, and housing issues on behalf of needy people.

- Child Care and Family Services—supports innovative public/private partnerships that offer programs to find childcare for people who work nontraditional hours.

- American Red Cross, International Red Cross, and Red Crescent Societies—provides annual contributions.

- Children's Miracle Network—raises funds for 170 affiliated children's hospitals in the United States and Canada. Most funds are raised through Marriott Pride which allows employees to participate at their hometown level.

- Habitat for Humanity International—contributes volunteer labor and funds to build decent affordable homes for people in need.

- America's Second Harvest—provides safe-to-donate food surpluses to more than 200 food banks and food rescue programs throughout the country.

- United Way—provides corporate support and has a long tradition of employee participation.

- Spirit to Serve Our Communities Day—a day in May of each year when Marriott honors employees during Associate Appreciation Week when associates volunteer to work on special projects that are beneficial to the community.

- Environmentally Conscious Hospitality Operations (ECHO)—a companywide program to "reduce-reuse-recycle" as much material and resources as possible. It also includes planting trees, cleaning beaches, and participating in other environmentally beneficial practices.

McDonald's Corporation

"We have an obligation to give back to the communities that give us so much."
(Ray Kroc, McDonald's founder)

McDonald's Corporation is the largest food service organization in the world. It numbers more than 30,000 units in over 120 countries and serves almost 50 million people each day. Approximately one-third of McDonald's stores are owned and operated by women and minorities. "Socially responsible leadership" is part of the company's mantra. McDonald's is an active community leader in terms of the corporation, its franchises, and the Ronald McDonald House Charities (RMHC). *Worth* magazine gives RMHC a high ranking in its list of "100 Best Charities in America."

The Ronald McDonald Houses exist to provide care and comfort for families who are away from home due to the hospitalization of their child or children. There are over 200 Ronald McDonald Houses in 20 countries around the world, providing a magnificent service at an extremely reasonable cost.

As a company, sports sponsorship, the environment, medicine, and education, among other venues, attract their interest.

SPORTS SPONSORSHIP

McDonald's operates a major scholarship program for children of its employees. It sponsors the McDonald's All-American High School Basketball Game, for both boys and girls each year, and it cosponsors the Powerade/McDonald's All-American High School Soccer Games.

ENVIRONMENT

McDonald's has formed an Animal Welfare Council that undertakes initiatives to provide for the well-being of cattle, poultry, and hogs. It has been a leader in recycling efforts of both paper products and aluminum can snap tops.

MEDICAL

RMHC has contributed millions of dollars to Interplast and Operation Smile, organizations that provide help with facial reconstruction and surgery. RMHC is also a million-dollar contributor to efforts to eliminate maternal and neonatal tetanus, a disease that claims the lives of 600 infants per day in developing countries. Additionally, numerous Ronald McDonald Care Mobiles provide pediatric care by traveling to children's locations, so these children do not have to go to hospitals.

Healthy Families of America, a program designed to prevent and treat child abuse, is a beneficiary of RMHC grants, as is the American Refugee Committee, which helps families with medical, educational, and financial needs due to civil strife.

EDUCATION

- RMHC has established several scholarship programs for minorities including:
  - RMHC/African-American Future Achiever
  - RMHC/Hispanic-American Commitment to Educational Resources
  - RMHC/UNCF Medical Scholars Program
  - RMHC/Asian Students Increasing Achievement
- RMHC sponsors Teacher of the Year Award programs and provides educational resources, such as textbooks and videos, to grade school and high school classrooms on subjects such as science, nature, wildlife, nutrition, and immunization.

McDonald's franchisees also have a culture and history of community involvement and support. Many McDonald's units have Playlands and PlayPlaces as part of their physical facilities. They provide disaster aid in times of hurricanes, earthquakes, and tornadoes, and sponsor little league teams, art and science exhibits and competitions, free food or gift certificates for local charitable projects, and scholarships for the children of their employees.

The foregoing community involvement program is not an exclusive listing of all that this organization does. Activists supporting different causes often target McDonald's for derision and unmerited criticism; in our view, it is a responsible, leading organization not only in its industry but also in the broader field of commerce.

Metropolitan Life Insurance Company N.Y.

"Our goals are to strengthen communities, promote good health and improve education."
(excerpt from the MetLife Foundation)

New York-based, 136-year-old MetLife is one of the largest insurance companies in the world. In addition to its proud history and solid financial structure, the company is known for its use of the MetLife blimp and its affiliation with Snoopy, the lovable and laughable dog character from the well-known cartoon *Peanuts*.

MetLife has an extensive corporate citizenship program and has supported merit-worthy programs for years in a meaningfully significant manner. The following is a representative sample of their largesse:

HEALTH

- National AIDS Fund
- Alzheimer's Association
- Awards for Medical Research (AMR) (also Alzheimer's related)
- Centers for Disease Control (CDC)
- Preventive Medicine Institute (PMI)
- Phoenix House Foundation (substance abuse prevention)

EDUCATION

- The MetLife Survey of the American Teacher—annual survey on the educational relationships and societal impact of current issues.
- Education Commission of the States (ECS)—helps modernize state educational systems.

- The Teachers Network—identifies and connects innovative teachers who exemplify professionalism and creativity within their public school systems.

- National Association of Secondary School Principals (NASSP)—assists principals in building family involvement in schools.

- The Community College Leadership Program (at the University of Texas)—launched the MetLife Foundation Initiative for Student Success to examine and promote practices that lead to student retention in college.

CIVIC AFFAIRS

- Enterprise Foundation—promotes effective management of affordable housing.

- Boys & Girls Clubs of America—provides constructive activities and adult supervision for disadvantaged youths after school.

- Trust for Public Land—creates and improves urban parks and playgrounds nationwide.

- Contributes to the National 4-H Council's Youth in Action/Community Service Grant Program.

- Contributes to the National Urban League.

CULTURE

- YouthARTS Resource Initiative—supports arts-related programs designed specifically for at-risk youth (numerous organizations received grants).

- Arts Education—funds grants for theater, dance, music, painting, and sculpting programs in cities around the nation.

- Awards for Cultural Excellence—recognizes programs of excellence at children's museums.

- American Symphony Orchestra League—recognizes programs that can serve as models for orchestras of all sizes.

- Public Broadcasting—is the lead sponsor in the Live from Lincoln Center series which features the finest in performing arts.

- Traveling Exhibits—supports on-the-road exhibits such as *Alice's Wonderland, The Color Yellow, Beauford Delaney* (African-American artist), *Elder Grace: The Nobility of Aging, Memory, Face to Face: Dealing with Prejudice and Discrimination*, and *Pictures Tell the Story: Ernest C. Withers* (African-American photographer).

- National Dance Tours—supports tours including the American Ballet Theater Company, Ailey II, Ballet Hispancio, Paul Taylor Dance Company, and the Pilobolus Dance Theater.

- Museums Connection Program—brings museums and communities closer together.

Microsoft Corporation

"Driven by the belief that amazing things happen when people get the resources they need, Microsoft has been using technology to spark the potential in individuals and communities since 1983."

(excerpt from Community Affairs)

Founded in 1975 as a small software company, Microsoft has expanded to become the largest company in its industry. It is involved in every aspect and type of software available today, from programming languages and operating systems to internet services and games. The company currently employs more than 50,000 people and operates in more than 50 countries. Its services are offered the world over. The founder, Bill Gates, and his partner, Paul Allen, began with the idea of having "a computer on every desk and in every home." At the time this was seen as a fantasy, but over the years it has become a reality. Gate's and Allen's early vision has helped change the way we communicate, do business, and live.

The first version of Microsoft Office was introduced in 1989, and it has been continually updated. In 1990, the first version of Microsoft Windows was released. In 2000, the company entered the market with Microsoft.net, its own platform. Microsoft has enjoyed incredible success, which can be measured by its continued progress and sustained leading position.

Microsoft has been a leader not only within the market, but also in the communities it serves. Its focus on the community is evidenced in its corporate mission: "To enable people and businesses throughout the world to realize their full potential." Microsoft operates an Employee and a Corporate Giving Program. The Corporate Program is focused on four main areas: access to technology, strengthening nonprofits, diversifying the IT workforce, and building communities. Each of these areas has a specific purpose:

- *Access to Technology:* The purpose of this area, which Microsoft offers through partnerships with other entities, is to provide access to necessary technology to underserved communities around the world.

- *Strengthening Nonprofits:* This area is aimed at helping nonprofit organizations become more effective and efficient in serving their customers and meeting their missions, through partnering with them and providing them with technology.

- *Diversifying the IT Workforce:* Microsoft furthers this goal through partnering with other organizations and supporting training and education in technology for those in underserved communities around the world.

- *Building Communities:* Microsoft's employees help to strengthen the communities in which they live and serve through giving and supporting diverse nonprofit programs and projects.

The Employee Giving Program is set up for employees to help through financial contributions, volunteered time, and donations of resources such as technical expertise. Microsoft offers a matching program in which the company will match individual charitable contributions, dollar-for-dollar, up to $12,000 annually for each employee.

Nordstrom, Inc.

"Nordstrom is committed to preserving the health and vitality of communities in which we do business."

(excerpt from the Community Service Statement)

John W. Nordstrom emigrated to the United States from Sweden in 1887. He worked at many different jobs before he was able to raise enough money to enter into a partnership with Carl Wallin, whom he had met while working in Alaska. From the very start, Nordstrom's business philosophy was based on exceptional service, selection, quality, and value.

In 1901, a young Nordstrom and partner Wallin opened their first store in Seattle, Washington. What began as a shoe store, Wallin & Nordstrom, has grown into a chain of full-service fashion emporiums known as Nordstrom department stores. Over the years, this company has flourished to become a nationwide fashion specialty chain. It is known for its impeccable service to its customers and its products of superior quality, with styles and sizes for all members of the family.

Nordstrom strongly values diversity and the importance of diversity to its workforce. Its commitment to maintaining a workforce representative of many backgrounds and to cultivating an environment where contributions from all parties are respected allows the company to enjoy great success both in business and in supporting their surrounding communities.

The recruitment and support of minorities and women has been an ongoing goal for Nordstrom, which seeks to increase the representation of minorities and women among its general employees as well as in management positions.

The corporation has enjoyed success in this regard and will continually seek to further this effort. Nordstrom also offers sensitivity training to its employees on a routine basis. This training focuses on diversity issues within the workplace.

The Supplier Diversity Program was created to support businesses owned by minorities and women. This program helps to enable these small companies and the communities in which they are located to achieve economic growth, and it ensures equal access to Nordstrom for all businesses, no matter the size.

As can be seen, Nordstrom is devoted to furthering diversity within the corporation and in its business relationships. The company sees this as a need that must be met at all levels of society. By pursuing diversity, Nordstrom tries to promote such practices within the society and the communities in which it serves.

Nordstrom is involved in many different activities in these areas, such as employment and promotion, training, community relations, and the Supplier Diversity Program. It supports many community organizations in many different ways. It financially contributes to efforts in education, human services, the arts, and community development.

Target Corporation

"The company seeks healthy, long-term growth by saving energy, increasing efficiency, reducing waste, and being respectful of our effect on the communities and eco-systems."

(excerpt from "About Target Corporation")

In 1961, Target was born out of a perceived need for less expensive goods sold in a more convenient format. Dayton's department stores noticed the demand for this offering, and one year later the first Target store was opened in Roseville, Minnesota. Since its opening in 1962, Target has experienced considerable growth and success. Today, the company is called the Target Corporation and is composed of many entities. Three of its retail divisions are Target, Marshall Field's, and Mervyns's; four of its other core businesses are Target Direct, Target Financial Services, Associated Merchandising Corporation, and Dayton's Commercial Interiors.

Within its three retail entities, the Target Corporation has something for everyone: ranging from upscale discount stores to full-scale department stores. Target's stores offer services such as Club Wedd wedding registry, Lullaby Club baby registry, and its own credit card called the Target Guest Card. In the 1990s, the Target Corporation opened the first Super Target store, which offers everything from groceries to clothing.

The Target Corporation has a strong commitment to the communities it serves. This commitment is mainly seen in the areas of diversity, the environment, and children.

DIVERSITY

The company's commitment to Equal Opportunity is seen on all levels of its business: employees, guests, and business. Target seeks to recruit and hire team members no matter what their differences are, as long as they do not interfere with effective job performance. As for guests, Target welcomes, respects, and seeks to make all guests comfortable in its shopping environment. The company also seeks equal opportunity by retaining a diverse workforce and developing products and services that reflect the diverse need in order to attain and retain an innovative advantage within the marketplace.

ENVIRONMENT

Target Corporation pays considerable attention to people and the planet. The company has focused efforts on recycling, package reduction, and energy conservation. Target has programs that recycle shopping carts, store fixtures, toner cartridges, guest bags, and in-store signage. Many of the company's products also are packaged in, or made of, recycled material. The products arrive at the stores with no excess packaging. If shoes arrive in boxes, they are made of material containing 80 percent recycled fiber. Target also has a program for recycling broken hangers. In 2001, Target Corporation's energy conservation program resulted in the savings of 37 million kilowatt-hours.

CHILDREN

The Target Corporation, in conjunction with the Tiger Woods Foundation, offers the Start Something Program to children ages 8–17. The program was created to help young people determine their life goals and what steps they should take to pursue them. The program consists of 10 two-hour sessions and is intended to be completed over a 10-week period. Recently the program has been implemented on line so that individuals may complete the program based on their own timetables. At the end of this program, the participants can apply for a scholarship to be used for anything that will help them achieve their goals. These scholarships are offered three times a year and range from $100 to $5,000.

al-Mart Stores, Inc.

"Wal-Mart's GOOD WORKS community involvement program is based on the philosophy of operating globally and giving back locally . . . . 100 percent of our funding initiatives are channeled directly into local communities by associates who live there."

(Wal-Mart-GOOD WORKS philosophy)

Founded in the 1960s, Wal-Mart Stores is the world's largest retailer with over $220 billion in sales, one million employees, and 1,100 units around the world. Founded by the legendary Sam Walton, the Bentonville, Arkansas, company has enjoyed meteoric growth in the years since its incorporation.

Accompanying that growth has been a well-orchestrated community outreach program of considerable magnitude. The following is a sampling of the types of activities the firm supports.

- Teacher of the Year award programs in each state culminate in the selection of a National Teacher of the Year.

- Supports America's Promise, an organization that conducts Groundhog Job Shadow Day, in which the company also participates. In this program, students shadow adults in the world of work to learn about different occupations.

- Provides scholarship funds for or through:
  - United Negro College Fund
  - League of United Latin American Citizens
  - University of Texas Pan American
  - Hispanic Association of Colleges and Universities
  - Higher REACH—for nontraditional students who have been employed by Wal-Mart for at least one year
  - Sam Walton Community Scholarship
  - Wal-Mart Associate Scholarships
  - Walton Family Foundation Scholarship

- Participates in the Jobs for American Graduates (JAG) program.

- Supports the Students in Free Enterprise (SIFE) program.

- Strongly supports Children's Miracle Network.

- Participates in CODE ADAM, a program to find missing children in company stores.

- Strongly supports the Missing Children's Network.

- Provides eye examination and glasses to needy children through Project Insight.

- Makes Community Matching Grants by matching funds raised by nonprofit groups in their communities.

- Supports Habitat for Humanity.

- Supports the United Way—by matching the contributions of its employees.

- Contributes to community literacy programs.

- Through Operation Uplink, the company issues telephone cards to members of the armed forces serving abroad so they can call home for free.
- As part of its Holiday Charity Program, each Wal-Mart store sponsors a day during the holiday season wherein a percentage of sales is donated to a local charity selected by the store.
- Supports National Grandparents Day by providing $300 per store to a local youth group which has a project that benefits senior citizens.
- Through its Volunteerism Always Pays (VAP) program, the company makes a charitable donation to nonprofit organizations where associates volunteer their time.
- During Wal-Mart Earth Day, stores invite local environmental organizations to their Earth Day Fair to set up exhibits to inform the community about environmental issues important to all of us.
- Kids For A Clean Environment (Kids F.A.C.E.) informs children of the importance of protecting the environment.
- Provides grants to nonprofit organizations that address environmental issues.

Epilogue

We started our journey of leadership exploration with an initial focus on the individual. People *do* make the difference.

We believe it is imperative to match the right type of leader with the appropriate stage of an organization's development to insure its sustainability. Organizations have life cycles just as people do, but organizations enjoy the benefit of having the ability to reinvent themselves. Successful leaders and organizations are mortal but can achieve immortality in history.

Organizations have leadership roles and responsibilities over and above the responsibilities of the individuals in an organization. Rising into a leadership position usually requires one or more leverage points for the organization and the right kind of leader at each step along the way. It is a competitive world and successful organizations have mastered both their internal and external focus.

In addition, by remaining in touch with the human spirit, often referred to in North America as the "American Way," successful organizations give back to the community from which they draw their success.

Still, with all that we know about successfully leading an organization, the subject of "leadership" is still discussed and debated throughout the world. At the individual level we often can detect leadership, or the lack thereof, when we see it, even though we may not comprehend or relate all the factors bearing on it.

As organizations move to a certain place in their life cycle, mistakes are still made by installing the "wrong kind" of leader at the helm; we all know "the right person at the right time" can propel an organization forward rapidly.

Organizations continually search for new and stronger leverage points so they can break away from the pack. Many stumble along the way.

In conclusion, irrespective of all the benefits organizations provide to their communities, relatively little recognition comes their way. In fact, often the larger and/or more successful an organization becomes, the more criticism it engenders. While some criticism is no doubt merited, we believe there is an imbalance of criticism over recognition, selfishness over altruism, indifference over appreciation, and suspicion over righteousness. It's time to turn that around!

I've been a follower! I've been a leader! Leadership is best!

William P. Fisher, Ph.D.

Leadership is not always taking others where they want to go. It's taking them where they need to go.

Christopher C. Muller, Ph.D.

Index